A GUIDE TO
heraldry

Herald is my name of old,
From which my metier may be told.
Aneas Sylvius* later on related
How the heralds were incorporated
Many years before to go on missions
Visiting princes and men of high position,
And freely passing every frontier.

Epigram by Hans Guldenmundt, about 1550
* Pope Pius II (1548–1564)

OTTFRIED NEUBECKER

A GUIDE TO

Heraldry

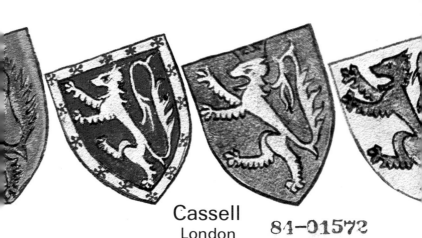

Cassell
London

CASSELL LTD.
35 Red Lion Square, London WC1R 4SG
and at Sydney, Auckland, Toronto,
Johannesburg,
an affiliate of
Macmillan Publishing Co., Inc.,
New York.

Conception and Design: Robert Tobler

A McGraw-Hill Co-Publication

In tourneying, the crested helmet
was only put on at the last moment.
The squire brought the helmet to his
knight. With his right hand the knight
held his lance with pennant and
guided his horse; with his left hand
he raised the helmet for all to see.

First published in Great Britain 1981

ISBN 0 304 30751 3

Printed and bound by: Brepols, Turnhout, Belgium
Composition by: Basler Zeitung, Basel, Switzerland
Photolithography by: Actual, Biel, Switzerland

Printed in Belgium

CONTENTS

ORIGINS
OF HERALDRY

In 1095 a rousing cry went up in Christendom, a call to take up the cross and set off to liberate the holy places. Few people, however, had any idea of the painful and dangerous adventure ahead. Now the relatively rough-hewn Europeans received a considerable surprise when they came up against an advanced culture and a technology based on scientific principles, as well as advanced techniques of war. They drew certain lessons from this, though largely only in relation to technology.

It became necessary to have better protective armor, in particular more extensive coverage of the face, and this had the effect of making the soldier unrecognizable. A further consequence was that, exactly like a present-day tank driver or aircraft pilot, the soldier had to decorate his outer covering with some easily identifiable sign.

This could take the form of some addition to his helmet, but it could also be painted on some part of his armor such as the shield or the horse trappings. A vassal at that time usually had to provide his own horse when going to war.

The crusaders attempted to graft their own social structure onto the areas they had won. They created a ruling upper class which applied the rules of feudalism more perfectly than at home, but because it was only an upper stratum it was that much more fragile.

The combination of several different elements laid the foundation stone of a phenomenon which embraced the whole of the civilized world as known to the Europeans. This phenomenon was armory, which as a result of its later manifestations is also called heraldry.

Feudalism was based on an unbreakable relationship

of mutual loyalty in which the vassal served his lord, and the latter provided him with care and protection. This feudal relationship was established for life between the king or his near subordinate and an individual. It terminated only with the death of one of the parties.

If the feudal lord was an institution, such as the Church, the question could arise of whether or not the death of that institution's representative, who might be a bishop, would dissolve the feudal relationship. The understandable desire of a vassal to secure the advantages of a feudal benefice for his descendants led inevitably to the principle of the inheritability of a fief. In a society which was not as yet oriented toward technical progress and a money economy, the basis of existence was agriculture and husbandry—the land. The migrations following the breakup of the Roman Empire brought profound changes in the distribution of property, which tended to work in favor of those in power. As a result, two types of property ownership arose in central Europe. The first was the *allodium*, which was the inherited possession of land belonging entirely to its owner. And the second type was the *feudum*, a piece of land or territory which belonged to the king or a high-ranking lord, but was leased by the latter to a vassal so that he could produce his means of subsistence and fulfill the duties incumbent on him as a feudatory tenant. In a time when might tended to be right, one of his main duties was to be ready to support the feudal lord in the military pursuit of his ends, in person or by any other means.

So long as such operations were undertaken by relatively small groups of

King Richard I effortlessly subdues an evil-looking Saladin, to whom the artist has given an imaginary shield.

armed men, the need for specific badges was not great; any kind of distinguishing sign would do. However, the situation immediately became different with the first Crusade, when men prepared to fight set out from all parts of Europe and found themselves forced to make common cause with neighbors from the same continent, but at the same time needed to keep close to their own countrymen. A sense of national consciousness was revealed, or at least encouraged, by the use of different colored signs of the cross, and at the same time the military leaders brought their feudal attitudes to the new situation. A badge of nationality was a boon for all those who after leaving their native land encountered a language barrier which could only be surmounted by the learned with the help of Latin. Even French, the main language of the educated, was little help, although it played an important role in the East.

The wholly personal relationship between the lord and his vassal also explains why in the early centuries of heraldry it was considered important that a coat of arms should indicate a particular person and not a

family. A young man of knightly birth made his entry into active life not through his father but through the sponsor who made him into a knight. It was the success of the feudatories in gradually making the fief inheritable which lent a degree of permanence to the coat of arms, by now becoming a genuine symbol.

The rules developed during the first few centuries of the second millennium A.D. were formulated and carried out by an increasingly important body of professionals, the heralds. And these same rules have remained valid with very little alteration to this day. While arms can look back on a history of several centuries, heraldry itself is permanently valid.

All political developments have made themselves felt through heraldic forms. This can best be observed at the foundation of a new state, which will hoist a flag with solemn ceremony on the first day of its independence. Soon after, it will communicate to friendly nations its future coat of arms, as well as the badges of its national airline and air force.

The increasing independence of the lower administrative orders and smallest population groups has a natural consequence in the creation of local arms. In such democratically constituted countries as Switzerland and Finland, therefore, almost every community has an heraldically irreproachable coat of arms.

Despite all adverse comment, this tendency has also affected families which regard themselves as pillars of their community and wish to contribute to its cohesion. The idea that one must be an emperor or a prince to bear arms has really been overcome now, and there is an increasing demand for coats of arms from families with a strong sense of identity and also from self-confident individuals.

For this reason,
everything connected with arms is called "heraldic,"
and the whole complex
of armorial knowledge and art is called
HERALDRY.

Arms represent people or groups of people
as though they
themselves were present.
The presence of a coat of arms acts as a substitute
for the person,
even after his death.

the herald

What is a herald, and where does the use of the term "heraldry" for the science of arms come from? There is no obvious connection between arms and heralds, and the term "heraldry" has only been in existence for some three hundred years. In fact a herald is a messenger and maker of proclamations. His task is, in the German phrase, *des Heeres zu walten,* to "manage the troops," presumably by proclaiming the commander's orders. This would seem to be the origin of the Old High German term *hariwalt,* which gradually penetrated all the European languages via the Old French form *herault.* In French poetry it appeared as early as 1285 in the form *hirau,* but the current German term *Herold* and English "herald" appeared a century later.

The close relationship between insignia and heralds arose naturally from the way medieval armies were organized and from the nature of

In the ancient world, the powers of individual gods were carefully allotted; the chief god, or father of the gods, needed a mediator to proclaim his heavenly will. In ancient Egypt, the sacred bull Apis *(above)* served as the herald of Ptah, the highest of the gods.

Right. In the famous *Livre des Tournois* of King René, there is a description of how the tournament is opened by the heralds. Those with the loudest voices had to call out three times: *"Or oyez, or oyez!"* ("Hear ye, hear ye!"), which was followed by the announcement of the individual contest.

12

medieval warfare. Feudal society was constantly embroiled in feuds which were conducted according to chivalrous ritual and ended with the loser having to pay hugely, in both land and property. Each

bility of the heralds. And the latter, who previously, as little more than messengers, had been included among the minstrels and other camp followers, now became persons of consequence whose advice

participant in a passage of arms, whether of a warlike or merely sporting character, wore a coat of arms on his shield, helmet, and banner, and on the trappings of his horse. This was the only means of distinguishing him from other combatants. Consequently there had to be someone who could read these signs and tell friend from enemy.

Within a few decades after the first insignia appeared, their use had spread so rapidly that knowledge of them and their functions became a responsi-

had to be taken. The first recorded presence of a herald at a battle was in July 1173, when according to the chronicler Guillaume le Maréchal a herald observed the Battle of Drincourt in Normandy. But this was still only an isolated case, attended by special circumstances, and the institution was slow in adoption. English documents from the year 1290 mention a "king of heralds" in the royal service. Some forty years later we find the first official appointment of the kind which was later to become general for all heralds, when a man named Andrew was given the official title of "Norroy" (North King). At that time, ordinary men did not have family names but only used Christian names. Those in royal service, however, could be raised from the crowd by the use of official designations which in themselves formed a special hierarchy. Thus the heralds were elevated from the level of servants, minstrels, and entertainers. At their head stood a king-at-arms or king of the heralds, followed by the heralds a step below and then by pursuivants (from the

Connétable (probably dating from the year 1309) describe these functions exactly, giving a vivid picture of the activity of the heralds of the time. The *Connétable*, whose office persisted until its abolition by Richelieu in 1627, was commander-in-chief of the army of the king of France.

The extensive knowledge of people required of the heralds demanded not only a good memory but also aids to memory in the form of written records. A truly systematic arrangement was unknown at the time, however. Summaries were drawn up according to

The duke of Brittany hands his king-at-arms the sword which the latter is to take to an opponent, to challenge him to a tournament. A pursuivant holds his master's cap and heraldic staff.

They show him eight imaginary coats of arms on a roll of parchment. These represent umpires, of which he may choose four.

The umpires wear their arms on badges fastened to their head-gear. A loud-voiced pursuivant *(right)* proclaims the start of the tournament.

French *poursuivant*, a candidate for office). Their functions were clearly defined.

In France the statutes for the

the numbers of followers a knight possessed, his appearance at military parades or coronations, and other indi-

The lodgings of the dukes of Brittany and Bourbon and their companions at a tournament, decorated with their banners and coats of arms (after the tournament book of King René).

cations of his position in the military hierarchy. Other systems were also used, such as the arrangement of the different coats of arms by individual districts, particularly in England where in the following centuries the science of heraldry was subjected to an especially rigid form of classification.

Military requirements not only made it necessary for the heralds to compile lists, but also imposed certain rules on their public conduct and way of life. They had to be able to cross the opponent's lines with impunity in a private feud or in a war and enter the enemy camp. They therefore wore an unmistakable costume consisting of an armorial surcoat, such as their lord himself wore on festive occasions, but—and

Ladies were naturally expected to play their role in these colorful proceedings. According to King René, they should be led four times past the helmets of the participants, which were placed in a row so that none might be overlooked. If any of the wearers had been heard to make disparaging remarks about the women, a lady would touch his helmet to single him out, and he would be called to account.

A herald meets Death. He wears the tabard of the margrave of Baden, bearing the arms of Baden (or a bend gules) and Sponheim.

Der dot   Der wapendreger

this was an important difference—without sword, dagger, or staff; a coat of mail was worn underneath in battle.

So long as the feudal system of war service remained, whereby princes, knights, and conscripted vassals were rec-

If a princely decree had to be made known, the herald would don his tabard. A trumpeter would assemble the

The unestablished, "freelance" heralds decorated their tabards with small plain armorial shields, while those officials with tabards bore the arms of their lords. On unimportant occasions the arms frequently took the form of a small pendant shield, such as was also worn by couriers carrying dispatches across the country.

The "Sicily" Herald *(far right)* served the king of Aragon (to whom Sicily then belonged) around 1420.

ognized by the standards round which they gathered, the heralds, were indispensable in every country in western Europe. They had always to remain close to their lord and be ready at any time of the day or night, especially in time of war. They were therefore quartered in the prince's tents.

prince's followers with three blasts on his horn. The herald would then read out the text of the decree to the assembled company.

Again wearing his tabard, he had to announce a truce if so ordered and bear messages to enemy commanders, to challenge them to fight, to demand that a fortress be given up, or to start negotiations for a surrender. He also had to organize individual combats between opposing members of the opposing camps.

He could be sure of a considerable reward from the enemy leader who received his news, especially if he appeared to be the kind of man who could keep his mouth shut. On his return, a herald was not supposed to utter a word about what he had seen of the enemy's preparations, for an

When battle was opened in a correct and chivalrous fashion, it was the custom to dub new knights before the beginning of the fighting, and the heralds had to be present as witnesses at the ceremony. In 1547, Hainault Herald witnessed and recorded that on the morning of the Battle of Mühlberg, the emperor Charles V dubbed Peter von Brandenburg knight. The reward to the herald for such attendance consisted of all the non-military equipment of the

ambush as an example. In fact he had to act as if he had seen nothing at all. Otherwise he would be looked upon as a spy—though many a pursuivant must have preferred this to letting his lord come to harm. At the same time he was allowed to give his lord useful advice, without details.

former esquire, which could however be redeemed with a mark of silver.

Everyone must have been aware before a battle that he might not come out of it alive. One of the functions of the heralds was therefore to record last wishes, take care of valuables, and also take note of

The herald represented on this play-
ing card wears the arms of Bohemia
as a badge.
The badge with the bear is that of the
Weibel of the valley of Ursern in
Switzerland.

physical characteristics by
means of which they could
identify the fallen. John Tal-
bot, Earl of Shrewsbury, fell in
1453 at the Battle of Castillon,
which ended the Hundred
Years' War between England
and France. The body of Tal-

which he felt by putting a fin-
ger in his master's mouth. A
touching scene, as related by
Mathieu d'Escouchy, took
place over the body when the
herald, finally convinced his
lord was dead, leaned over and
kissed him on the mouth. In

The pursuivant of the elector
Frederick II of Brandenburg (1413–
1471). The one-armed pursuivant of
the tourneying society "Ass," Hans
Ingeram, represented himself and his
own coat of arms in the armorial
which he compiled in 1459.
A Spanish herald from the last years
of the reign of King Ferdinand I
(d. 1516).

bot was so mutilated as to be
unrecognizable and had already begun to decompose.
His herald could only identify
him by a gap in his teeth,

tears, the herald declared that
his forty years of service were
at an end. To symbolize this he
took off his tabard and laid it
on the body.

The heralds of Great Britain were present at the coronation of Queen Elizabeth II on 2 June 1953, contributing to the pageantry of the occasion with their splendidly colored and richly embroidered tabards *(below)*.

Heralds were unarmed and in principle were not to be taken prisoner. As soon as the battle had begun, they had to move some distance away, but not too far from their lord's banner, and follow the progress of the fighting by watching the coats of arms: they also had to observe and report on the behavior of the combatants, including any acts of cowardice which they saw. After the armies had disengaged, the heralds of both sides would go onto the battlefield to decide between them who was the victor of the day. The side with the largest number of dead was considered defeated.

Because of their exact eye-witness knowledge of events, the heralds were a valuable source of information to chroniclers and illustrators about these often historically decisive battles. The heralds of the losing side usually went to the enemy commander, congratulated him on the victory which God had granted him, and begged him to ask God's mercy for the souls of those killed in action. In addition they could render certain services to the victor: after the Battle of Agincourt in 1415, "Mountjoie," the king-at-arms of the king of France, was requested by the king of England, Henry V, to declare him victor and tell him the name of the neighboring

Initial with a portrait of Garter King of Arms John Smert. From an initial letter of a grant of arms made by him in 1456.

castle. This was done, and King Henry, according to the prevailing custom, announced that the battle would be named after the castle.

Once the fighting was over the heralds also had the lengthy task of making lists of those killed, as identified by their coats of arms. They also had to arrange for burials.

As a sign of victory, the heralds had immediately to raise the standard of their lord and make sure that the banners of the loser were handed over. And as they could not themselves be victorious in battle and share the booty, they were to receive a fully furnished house instead, or its equivalent in money. The high regard and privileges attached to their position often attracted untrustworthy people. Thus the French kings-at-arms once had to ask their king to forbid tradespeople to pass themselves off as heralds as a means of evading taxes.

Exemption from taxes was only one of the heralds' privileges. Another was the freedom to travel where they wished. This enabled them to undertake long journeys during which they could increase their knowledge of foreign lands and armory. Many of them recorded what they saw in words and pictures, and it is to this practice that we owe the armorial collections on which our knowledge of medieval heraldry is chiefly based.

TABARD OF THE BURGUNDIAN HERALD
FOR THE DUKEDOM OF LUXEMBOURG

TABARD WITH THE FULL ARMS OF SPAIN

23

SOURCES FOR THE STUDY
OF HERALDRY

Heralds gathered their knowledge of the arms in actual use as organizers of tournaments and other assemblies of knights. They noted down in lists what they saw, aiming for completeness only as far as the particular occasion required. Hence this type of list was called an "occasional roll" in England. Also in England, official requirements produced the so-called ordinaries, which are arranged according to the charges on the shield and not according to the name of the lord or lords represented by the arms. England is far richer than any other country in armorial collections of this kind. In the rest of Europe, ordinaries were made up almost solely for learning purposes, showing examples of different charges. No great interest was shown in them until the nineteenth century and the results of research are still shamefully small. Nevertheless, in the last few decades the scientific evaluation of medieval armorial collections of all kinds has made considerable progress.

There has been a general tendency to include with armorial collections other sources which do not strictly deserve this name. Such sources are illustrated manuscripts, often lavishly decorated with coats of arms. Such illustrations are useful to us today, but we need to distinguish between arms which can be considered genuine and arms which were invented as purely decorative elements.

In addition to those forms of armorial collections so far described, there are those works which record the membership of a corporation. Perhaps not the first, but by far the most

The Zurich armorial roll makes a clear distinction between arms connected with persons and purely territorial signs. The former consist of shields, helmets, and crests, and the latter are represented by banners.

Right: A page from the so-called *Wijnbergen Armorial* which assembles the first twenty-five of the sixty-four arms of the march of Artois.

Eustace de neulle . b.

gilles de nem le . b.

stace de ne le .

pierre de neulle .

Aymer de neulle .

Iehan de la haie . b.

breng de la haie .

han de la haie

Iehan de cen silles . F.

le ploumen de croisilles .

le chastelem daruus

baudouyn de hachicourt . b.

michiel de

Iehan de

significant examples for the time, are the books of the Brotherhood of St. Christopher at Arlberg.

Where such a brotherhood stretched over a wide area, heraldically illustrated works appeared in many places. There were lists of members of a profession, donors of requiems and vassals, and even university matriculation registers, many of remarkable artistic quality. Such celebrated orders of knights as the Order of the Garter and the Order of the Golden Fleece, of

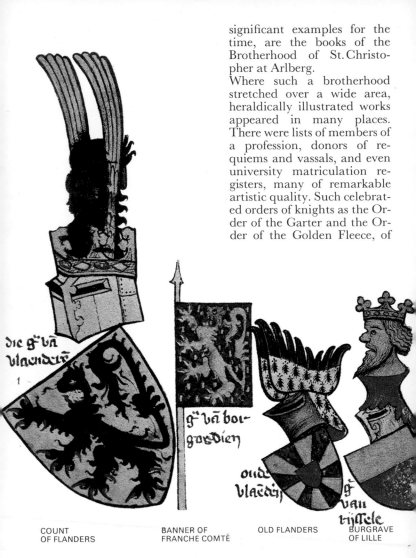

COUNT
OF FLANDERS

BANNER OF
FRANCHE COMTÉ

OLD FLANDERS

BURGRAVE
OF LILLE

In the *Armorial de Gelre,* the arms of the vassals of a great lord are arranged in a row beside his own arms. They have the partly imaginary crest consisting of a curious panel opening out into a feathered end like a wing.

Hubertus and of St. Michael, could afford particularly expensive and outstandingly produced armorial books. One particularly fine work is *Bruges'*

26

Garter Book, which contains representations of the oldest knights of the Garter. Armorial books of this kind relating to the membership of an order can still be found today.

Armorial collections can be technically divided into rolls and books according to their form; their use, however, varies. The term "roll," which is derived from a roll of parchment, has been kept up to the present day to designate a register with a more or less official character, as in the term "roll of trademarks."

material is as great as that of similar arms painted on paper or parchment.

The use of coats of arms as a means of enlivening historical or mythical accounts seems to have been more popular among the Germans than in other countries. In any case, up to this point the heraldic literature of other countries contains only armorial collections, and no chronicles with heraldic illustrations are to be found. One important exception is the chronicle of the Englishman Matthew Paris

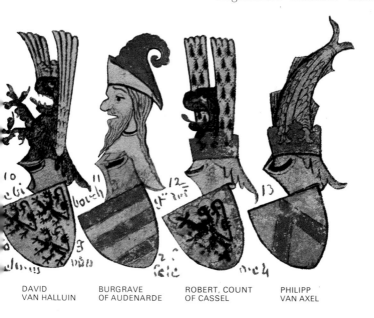

DAVID
VAN HALLUIN

BURGRAVE
OF AUDENARDE

ROBERT, COUNT
OF CASSEL

PHILIPP
VAN AXEL

Items such as furniture and tapestries decorated with coats of arms may also be included among armorial collections. Their value as source

(d. 1259). It contains the oldest existing record of the different families of knights, illustrated in color. The author gives the double eagle as the sign of the

27

The arms of Scotland are essentially the same as those used today.

German empire at a time when this had yet to be established.

The so-called *Balduineum*, which describes the emperor Henry VII's journey to Rome, is a valuable heraldic source and has been the subject of extensive research. Its most heraldically significant features are the representation of Henry before, during, and after his crowning as emperor; the still unexplained elongated red and yellow pennant, which accompanies the march to Rome (possibly the badge of Patricius of Rome); and the fact that the author indicates by graphic means when he does not know a coat of arms, usually that of an opponent. The heraldically illustrated chronicles of a later date make useful source material because they contain the short-lived coats of arms used by many nobles but more particularly by members of the church. Arms such as these can be used to date other armorial collections, particularly by means of the frequently changed arms of the popes.

The chronicles of the fifteenth century, however, tend to lapse into fantasy. Excited by reports of journeys to foreign lands, the authors of armorial

The arms of France became stabilized in the first third of the fourteenth century as three fleurs-de-lis.

collections tended more and more to invent arms for the kings of distant countries; chroniclers invented coats of arms for the ancestors of their landlords, which have no interest as historical sources but appeal through the motifs chosen and the skill with which they are drawn. A distinction must be drawn between chronicles of this kind and the eye-witness reports of factual events.

A listing of the earliest known armorial items would begin with three thirteenth-century rolls from the Franco-Dutch area. The first, from 1254, is a notable testimony to the immunity of the heralds, embracing as it does the arms of both sides. There is some doubt as to whether the list of the tournament of Compiègne (1278) was the earliest of its kind. The authenticity of certain tournament lists from around the same period, such as that of a tournament at Cambrai in 1267, has also been questioned. The illustrated or written records of the arms of participants in a battle or siege are more interesting to the historical researcher than dubious tournament lists. We know of several from England, among them the roll or Caerlaverock. Quite unique are the arms of some German knights who were released from prison in Italy in 1361 after having sworn an oath to keep the peace. Being little skilled in reading and writing, they probably could not spell their names which, as a result, are garbled and Italianized. But they were able to identify themselves by their arms.

It was not only in a military context, however, that the herald was officially obliged to compile lists. Apart from the heraldic illustration of chronicles, we find the use of arms as decorative material in other literary accounts. Among these the "great Heidelberg song manuscript" (the *Manesse Codex*) is particularly noteworthy. In the manuscripts of the *Sachsenspiegel*, on the other hand, arms play only a subsidiary role, serving to illustrate points of justice.

In the late Middle Ages, arms were displayed in many places. Works of art decorated with arms possessed aesthetic charm as well as providing information on their historical context. Some of these deserve to be included in a list of armorial collections. Special

care appears to have been taken with the preparation and selection of arms included in the decorative friezes created for festive occasions such as a royal or princely visit. Examples are those produced for the "Zum Loch" house in Zurich and the tower at Erstfelden; for the castle of Rivoli; and for the armorial hall at Lauf, where Charles IV often stayed. There is also a table from the

King Edward the Confessor (reigned 1042—1066), the founder of Westminster Abbey. The arms which were subsequently attributed to him are based on one of his silver coins. Imaginary portrait from a copy of the *Rous Roll*.

30

This illustration from "the great Heidelberg song manuscript" shows Werner von Teufen ardently wooing a lady while engaged in falconry. His armorial shield shows the whole helmet and crest.

terested in heraldry. One such person was Ulrich von Richental, who went from house to house at the time and noted down what he saw, to include it in his chronicle of the council. Unfortunately he got his notes mixed up so that his account is generally confused, especially in that part which deals with the arms of the churchmen. In addition he was rather given to speculation and there are many coats of arms which he could not have noted down from a lodging house, but must have taken on trust from unreliable informants.

In his efforts at comprehensiveness, Ulrich von Richental was continuing a tradition unknown to him which was already a century and a half old. This was the production of armorial collections which aimed at universal validity. The urge to produce armorial collections was prompted by either pure cultural interest or professional necessity, and in talking of general armorial collections a distinction must be drawn between those of the heralds and those of private collectors or sponsors. Both kinds first appear about the middle of the thirteenth century.

town hall at Lüneburg which must have been decorated for some festive occasion with its allegorical medallions and coats of arms along the edges. The custom of using coats of arms to decorate one's dwelling has an important parallel in the central European custom of putting up one's arms on the outside of the inn or lodging where one stopped. Anyone who sought a quarrel would tear down the board displaying the arms—just as the plates outside present-day embassies are often damaged by rioting crowds.

A great congress like the Council of Constance (1414 to 1418) was a veritable mine of information for anyone in-

In mid-thirteenth century, Matthew Paris produced his chronicle *Historia Anglorum (History of the English)*. The first two shields show the arms of the king of England and his brother, Richard, Earl of Cornwall, who was elected king of Romans and crowned in 1257.

The collections of the private authors are of greater cultural interest than could be expected of those made by officials. The above-mentioned poetic portrayals of arms rank as literary creations, but over and above this it is precisely these private collections which emphasize the value of knowing the full armorial bearings, including crests on helmets. Helmet crests are included in the important armorial roll of Zurich, which is somewhat difficult to date—containing no arms of members of the clergy—and the armorial book *Van den Ersten*.

Most surviving armorials give the full armorial bearings or "achievement" of arms. The most important German armorial by a private collector is that of Konrad Grünenberg. Also a native of Constance, although he must have lived too late to know Ulrich von Richental personally, Grünenberg adopted the work of the latter and not only extended it but also collated it in a series of powerful drawings. In 1442, Grünenberg was appointed chief architect of his home town of Constance, and three times he was mayor. He finished his comprehensive work of heraldry on 9 April

1483, and three years later set off on a six-month pilgrimage to the Holy Land.

The armorial collections produced by heralds or other officials noticeably do not concern themselves with the helmet and crest until the middle of the fourteenth century. This applies even to England where crests were of a particularly extravagant nature, and still are. After that time, however, Continental heralds endeavored to record the complete arms; an outstanding example of this is the armorial of the "Gerle" herald, *Armorial de Gerle*. Albrecht of Bavaria, Count of Holland since 1390, later gave this herald the official name of "Bayern" (Bavaria). In addition he was king-at-arms of Ruyers.

The arrangement of the earliest heralds' armorial rolls shows clearly that they were designed for a specific purpose. There is little interest in comprehensiveness. Foreigners, even those of princely rank, tend to be included in appendices; family arms are arranged according to tourneying regions and the feudal hierarchy. In the fifteenth century the differences between collections start to disappear, but now the name of the herald who wrote a collection is given. The rolls are known by that name or, failing this, by a place name or perhaps the name of a previous owner, sometimes a person who did not even own the original, but merely a copy.

The invention of printing in the fifteenth century introduced into the production of armorial books first the use of a pre-printed template of shield, helmet, and helmet mantling, and then the art of copper-plate engraving.

Despite this new develop-

In the book of the Council of Constance, Ulrich von Richéntal included the arms of the abbots and abbeys subject to the bishop of Constance. Some of them added their own family arms to the arms of their abbey, using both the second and third positions of the quartered shield.

ment, interest continued in arms collections which were not intended for publication; witness the armorials of orders of knights which are maintained to the present day.

One splendid but final effort on the official side was the creation of the *Armorial Général* by an edict of Louis XIV in 1696. The former Juge Gé-Général (Keeper of the General Armorial), but at the same time made subordinate to a government official, Adrien Vannier. The purely fiscal motivation of the appointment and the disputes which arose from it in fact spoiled the whole undertaking. But in its benefits to heraldry, the event was of inestimable value.

In 1615, Louis XIII created the post of Juge Général des Armes de France, but it did little to help efforts at systematizing the bearing of arms in France. Louis XIV again raised the

N° 20.

PAR ORDONNANCE RENDUE le 17e du mois de Janvier de l'an 1695. par Mrs les Commissaires Généraux du Conseil députés sur le fait des Armoiries.

Celles de Gilles des Plasses, Marchand Drapier, Bourgeois de Paris.

Telles qu'elles sont ici peintes & figurées, après avoir été reçûes, ont été enregistrées à l'Armorial Général, dans le Régître cotté Paris, en conséquence du payement des droits reglés par les Tarif & Arrest du Conseil, du 20e de Novembre de l'an 1696. en foi dequoi, le présent Brevet a été délivré par Nous CHARLES D'HOZIER, Conseiller du ROI, & Garde de l'Armorial Général de France, &c. A Paris le 23e du mois d'Avril, de l'an 1698.

idea of registering arms, this time as a means of gaining extra revenue. In the meantime skilled engravers and printers had brought out printed armorials privately.

In principle, anyone may choose his own coat of arms. Not everyone takes advantage of this, but those who do, generally feel the need to have their choice ratified by the appropriate authority. The manner of this authorization depends on political circumstances. Monarchies have a stronger interest in the observation of social divisions than republics. They therefore tend to maintain the nobility as an institution, and usually have an office for issuing grants of noble status. In the German Roman Empire this was the Imperial Chancery where, from the fourteenth century onward, particular attention was also given to the graphic design of grants of arms. The conferment of titles was very formally expressed, together with the granting of arms, in documents known as patents of nobility. Letters Patent for the grant of arms were also issued to families who remained commoners. Initially such documents were on sheets of vellum, like those used in

Illustrated here are the arms of Alexander Vassilievich, Count Suvorov-Rimnikskii, which were granted him by the czar of Russia on 11 April 1791. The arms include the German imperial eagle, which had been conferred on him by the German Roman emperor Josef II. When Suvorov became a prince of the Russian empire in 1799, his arms were "bettered" and the Russian imperial eagle was added.

England to this day, but beginning in the eighteenth century they were issued in the form of a *libelle*, a small book. The patents of nobility issued during the final decades of the kingdom of Prussia, which perished in 1918, were also in book form. They were bound in leather, with the royal eagle embossed on the covers in color. The corners were decorated with silver plates, and the Great Seal of Prussia, made of red wax and enclosed in a protective silver capsule, was attached with a tasseled silver cord.

In England, Letters Patent for the grant of arms are to this day issued on sheets of vellum. In this open letter, addressed "To all and singular to whom these Presents shall come," three kings-at-arms inform the reader as to the authority of their office, the application made to them by the recipient, and the arms granted and assigned *(document at right)*. The document shows the new armorial ensigns, consisting of the arms, standard, and badges—in this case of Imperial Tobacco Limited. At the top are the royal arms flanked by those of the Duke of Norfolk as Earl Marshal and Hereditary Marshal of England and those of the College of Arms. In the right-hand margin are the arms of office of the three kings-at-arms issuing the Letter (Garter, Clarenceux, and Norroy and Ulster). These reappear in the seals attached to the signatures at the bottom. Other countries formerly also had armorial offices where warrants granting the right to use titles were issued or prepared for the monarch. In exceptional cases they also had authority to assign arms to commoners. Nowadays Letters Patent for the grant of arms are generally issued by professional associations.

TO ALL AND SINGULAR

to whom these Presents shall come Sir Anthony Richard Wagner, Knight Commander of the Royal Victorian Order, Garter Principal King of Arms, John Riddell Bromhead Walker, Esquire, Member of the Royal Victorian Order, upon whom has been conferred the Decoration of the Military Cross, Clarenceux King of Arms and Walter John George Verco, Esquire, Commander of the Royal Victorian Order, Norroy and Ulster King of Arms Whereas Richard Anthony Garrett Esquire, Captain (retired) the 22nd Dragoons, Chairman of did represent unto The Most Noble Bernard Marmaduke, Duke of Norfolk of the Most Noble Order of the Garter, Knight Grand Cross of the Royal Victorian Order, Knight Grand Cross Excellent Order of the British Empire, upon whom has been conferred the Territorial Decoration, Earl Marshal ary Marshal of England and One of Her Majesty's Most Honourable Privy Council, now deceased, that Imperial ited was incorporated as a limited Company on the Sixteenth day of February 1973 under the Companies 1967 That the Directors of the said Company are desirous of having Armorial Ensigns duly assigned to with lawful authority and he therefore as Chairman of the said Company and on behalf of the Direct- did request the favour of His Grace's Warrant for Our granting and assigning such Arms and Crest and in ent such Supporters and such four Devices or Badges as We may consider fit and proper to be borne & erial Tobacco Limited on Seals or otherwise all according to the Laws of Arms And forasmuch as the said d did by Warrant under his hand and Seal bearing date the Eighteenth day of December 1974 authorize s to grant and assign such Armorial Ensigns accordingly Know Ye therefore that We the said Garter, Cla- Norroy and Ulster in pursuance of His Grace's Warrant and by virtue of the Letters Patent of Our several ich of Us respectively granted do by these Presents grant and assign unto the Arms following that is to say:- Purpure a Bend lozengy Argent between two Coronets composed of o Flowers raised on points above a rim Or And for the Crest On a Wreath Or and Sable A demi Maiden per crowned with a Coronet as in the Arms Or vested Purpure garnished and holding before her a bunch Plants Or Flowered Argent. Mantled Purpure doubled Or, as the same are in the margin hereof more- ted And by the Authority aforesaid We do further grant and assign the following four Devices or Badges y:- (1) Three Coronets as in the Arms in triangle Or enclosing a Tobacco Flower Argent pierced Or Horns addorsed points downward Argent enfiled by a Coronet as in the Arms Or (3) An open Port- Towers Argent masoned Sable ensigned by a Coronet as in the Arms Or (4) The Bowl of a Tobacco Pipe n Annulet Argent its stem issuant from the sinister side thereof, as the same are also in the margin plainly depicted And by the Authority aforesaid I the said Garter do by these Presents further grant & the Supporters following that is to say:- On the dexter and on the sinister an Unicorn both Erminois attired unguled horned and armed the Unicorn also e and both gorged with Coronets as in the Arms Argent attached thereto Chains reflexed over their argin hereof more plainly depicted, the whole to be borne and used for ever hereafter by Imperial ited on Seals or otherwise according to the Laws of Arms In witness whereof We the said Garter, Cla- Norroy and Ulster Kings of Arms have to these Presents subscribed Our names and affixed the Seals of Offices this Thirtieth day of October in the Twenty fourth year of the Reign of Our Sovereign Lady Eliza- ond by the Grace of God of the United Kingdom of Great Britain and Northern Ireland and of Her other Territories Queen, Head of the Commonwealth, Defender of the Faith and in the year of Our Lord One ine hundred and seventy-five.

J.R.B. Walker   Clarenceux   Walter J. Verco   Norroy & Ulster

THE PRINCIPAL ELEMENTS
OF A COMPLETE ACHIEVEMENT

IMPERIAL BANNER (France)——
or oriflamme

TIP OF LANCE——

KING'S CROWN——

ARMORIAL BANNER——

DOME OF ARMORIAL TENT——
with motto

The consecutive arms of the former kingdom of Prussia provide an example of the changes that can take place on one coat of arms.

The shield *(below)* bears the arms created in 1701 for the new title of king.

The large achievement *(opposite)* brings together, as quarterings in one shield, the arms of fifty-two small ter-

The dome distinguishes an armorial tent from an armorial cloak. Armorial cloaks, too, are hitched up at the sides.

KING'S HELMET (visor right up)——

The colors of the mantling are those of the principal inescutcheon

ERMINE LINING——

Naturalistically represented in armorial cloaks

SUPPORTERS——

Wild men, girded and crowned with oak leaves

PRINCIPAL INESCUTCHEON——

The other inescutcheons and the 48 quarterings of the escutcheon, as well as the base (field of royal prerogative), are presented in hierarchic order. Another possibility would be a geographical arrangement.

ritories, dukedoms, and counties which the king of Prussia had considered worthy of being represented in his overall title. The savage men and other decorative motifs could be changed according to circumstances, or left out altogether.

The king of Prussia normally replaced the crest with a royal crown.

COMPARTMENT or CONSOLE——

The form of the compartment is usually only given in outline in a blazon. Ornamental foliage may replace the marble pedestal.

ORDERS ON THE COLLANE——

If there are several, the chain of the superior order forms the largest circle.

GOTT MIT UNS

H. Strahl

the shield

The shield has become most important as a basis for the display of what originally were simply called "signs" or badges. These later came to be regarded as heraldic devices and ordinary figures. Before this was to happen, however, the shield underwent centuries of development as a defensive and even an offensive weapon. In the *Sachsenspiegel*, the different feudal estates of the Middle Ages are described as *Heerschilde*—literally as "army shields." This indicates how far life in the Middle Ages was based on force.

When William, Duke of Normandy, afterward known as the Conqueror, crossed the Channel for England in 1066, his army consisted of mounted knights. The pictorial record of the Battle of Hastings on the famous Bayeux tapestry, and other scenes on this same work of art, show for the first time a shield which was henceforth to be known as the Norman shield. A distinction must be

The relationship between people and arms is expressed in the seals which exactly reproduced the heraldic escutcheon in its contemporary form, with the addition of an inscription referring to the bearer of the seal round the edge. Knight's seal showing Duke Bengt Birgersson of Sweden in full armor; 1282; original 77 mm. diameter.

Right: A knight's shield from Seedorf, a monastery founded in 1197 on the Lake of Lucerne. The silver lion on a blue ground represents the arms of the monastery's founder, Arnold von Brienz (d. 1225). The Seedorf shield is the only "Norman" shield which has survived. It has been modified by cutting off the upper rounded edge close to the lion's head to achieve the shape which had become fashionable around 1220.

41

made between small shields carried on the arm and large ones driven into the ground to make a wall. Around 1500, graphic considerations became all-important in their design.

Up to the fifteenth century, people were reluctant to carry armorial shields divided into more than four "quarters" or fields. Once, however, the decorative effect of armorial designs was recognized, they established a place for themselves in the fine arts.

Before setting out on the third Crusade, the kings of France (Philippe II) and England (Henry II) and Count Philip of Flanders met at Gisors in northeast France on 13 January 1188. They decided on particular colors for the crosses to be worn by their men. These were red for the French, white for the English, and green for the Flemish. After Henry II died, Richard I, Cœur de Lion, led the English participants in the Crusade. Every Crusader could now recognize, by the color of the cross worn by his fighting companion, what language he spoke. The Crusades were not the only military undertakings of the Middle Ages. Petty feuds

42

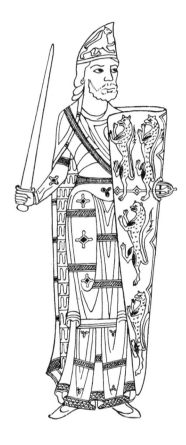

Full-length representation of Count Geoffrey of Anjou, called Plantagenet. King Henry I of England (reigned 1100—1135) gave his son-in-law Geoffrey a shield with several small lions on it. This is the earliest evidence of the transferring of arms from a man to his descendants.

Left: Japanese standing shields with archers kneeling behind. Detail from a colored woodcut.

and quarrels between neighbors filled the lives of a social class whose strength was based on the force of arms, which had therefore to be constantly exercised and tested. Pomp and circumstance also had their role, and military parades are held to this day. In the Middle Ages, the public taste for such spectacles was catered to by tournaments, which literary sources mention initially in the thirteenth century.

At first designed to test the fighting capabilities of the participants, the tournaments soon developed increasingly strict rules. Eventually these rules became so refined that the circle of people allowed to take part in tournaments was considerably restricted. It was the aim of the established nobility, whose members could show four noble ancestors, to bar the access of rising families to their closed society. In addition there was the condition that if a man wished to take part in a tournament, a member of the same family must have taken part in another tournament in the past fifty years. The ladies, for whose favor many rode in the lists, distributed the prizes. They made the tournaments a festive social occasion in which the highest social classes took part, often as fighters but even more often as spectators. It was essential for a young noble to prove himself in a tournament if he was to rise above esquire and become a knight.

A king dubs an esquire a knight after the latter has been given new clothing and his shield and banner. A light blow on the shoulder with a sword will be the last he may receive without responding.

In order to become a knight a man also had to have taken part in a campaign, which meant that he had to make a "journey" against an enemy. The need for some suitable "enemy" prevented many a peaceful settlement of petty feuds. In tournaments one did not compete against real enemies. The question of who were to be opponents was decided by lot among people of similar rank at the initial "distribution," which was combined with the inspection of helmets. At the same time the genealogy of the participants was checked, and people frequently were turned away. The list of those rejected is often astonishingly long in tournament books.

The pageantry developed in tourneying was by definition thoroughly heraldic in character. The heralds made sure that the heraldic rules were kept, rejected coats of arms which broke the rules of color, and demanded proof of the right to wear a crest with a crown on it, which usually required an imperial certificate. The lists drawn up by these organizers are sometimes also illustrated with arms and together form a valuable category among the occasional rolls. In the fifteenth century, tourneying reached the height of its development, only to decline very rapidly around the middle of the century.

The further development of heraldry was decisively influenced by various changes in tournament rules. In tourneying with a mace, instead of unseating one's opponent with a lance, one had to strike off his crest with the mace.

An announcement had to be made before each tournament as to which kind of tourneying was allowed. Under Emperor Maximilian numerous types were basically of three kinds —mace tourneying with club and sword in special half armor; tourneying proper, a full-scale fight with lance and sword in strengthened, cuirasses; and tourneying on foot with lance and sword in cuirasses.

Changes in the technology of weaponry caused the interest in tournaments to decline. In 1439 the tournament held at Landshut ended a long series. In 1479 the Frankish knights

ELONGATED TRIANGULAR
SHIELD WITH FAMILY ARMS,
2ND HALF OF 13TH CENTURY

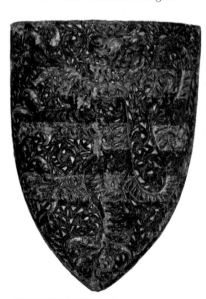

ORNAMENTAL SHIELD OF
LANDGRAVE HENRY OF THURINGIA,
LATE 13TH CENTURY

were conceived, including group battles which must have produced the most incredible mêlée. But the tournaments attempted to revive the practice, but the attempt ended eight years later with the last mace tournament at Worms.

By that time tourneying had become not only too expensive, but also useless as a form of practice. When events similar to tournaments were held in succeeding decades they were more correctly referred to as knightly games.

In the meantime gunpowder had been invented, though its use still presented some problems. Armaments technology in the fifteenth century was at first focused not so much on

cased in iron. The result was plate armor. This became increasingly artistic, increasingly mobile—thanks to skillfully constructed joints—but at the same time increasingly heavy.

The development of the kind of shield which survived in heraldry stems entirely from hand-to-hand fighting with sword and lance. The fact that sword strokes were directed chiefly at the enemy's head

STANDING SHIELD OF
THE TOWN OF ERFURT

JOUSTING SHIELD
BY TADDEO DI BARTOLO,
ITALIAN, CIRCA 1300

BURGUNDIAN PAVIS,
2ND HALF OF
15TH CENTURY

this as on the penetrating power of the crossbow. The soldier had to be fitted out like a shield himself, completely en-

had a decisive influence on the design of the helmet. The lance carried on horseback was aimed at the entire body

46

Another type to develop were large shields which could be placed side by side to form a protective wall in front of foot-soldiers or crossbowmen. As these pavés were used prin-

covering, but primarily at the vulnerable knee.

The classic triangular shield, named the "heater-shield" because in outline it resembles the base of a flatiron, could be smaller after the invention of the armored knee plate. But the basic shape remained the same.

Probably influenced by the practice of carrying a lance, a new form of shield appeared in the middle of the fourteenth century. We shall refer to this as a jousting shield to distinguish it from the triangular shield. A man might well possess both types. Its distinguishing mark was a sharp indentation in the top, to the right of the bearer, which served to support the lance and was known as a lance-rest or *bouche*. At first the jousting shield differed from the three-cornered shield only in outline. It was also painted with heraldic designs or decorated with relief patterns. But soon the surface of the jousting shield was painted with the full achievement of arms and even decorated with representations of whole scenes.

HORSE'S HEAD ARMOR BEARING THE ARMS OF THE EMPEROR FERDINAND I, AUGSBURG, 1558—1559

cipally by municipal defense forces, one finds whole sets of these shields in local museums in Germany and elsewhere.

The table on the right is based entirely on original sources, mostly seals and other clearly dated material. This makes it very useful for the dating of works of art. Initially, shields used for fighting and heraldic shields had the same form. When shields were no longer used in battle, the design became purely ornamental and largely architectonic.

The standing shield for a crossbowman with the arms of a Roman king from the house of Austria, of St. George's chivalry and the town of Winterthur, gives an idea of the extent to which heraldic designs can be mixed with ornamentation. It also demonstrates how the need for decoration always seems to predominate on articles of human warfare. The arms of the king of the Romans and St. George's chivalry enable the shield to be dated fairly accurately. The single-headed eagle was only used by the future emperor Frederick III before he was crowned, that is, before 1452. He was also the first emperor to superimpose his own family arms on the breast of the eagle. By his renewal of St. George's chivalry he also forged a tool which enabled him to combine family with imperial politics. The town of Winterthur at that time supported the Hapsburgs.

THE NETHERLANDS, including Belgium, provide some particularly early examples of heraldic development.

ENGLAND
In the Gothic period, the form of the armorial shield in the British Isles largely conformed to reality. The German *Tartsche* is usually referred to as a jousting shield. It is treated heraldically like other shields.

FRANCE
Here the classic form of shield has always prevailed, but stylistic changes have produced some lively examples.

GERMANY
Until around 1500, armorial shields in the German-speaking area matched the shield used for fighting. The knight's jousting shield had a strong influence in German heraldry.

ITALY
Italian heraldry introduced architectonic elements and typical forms into armorial art. Jousting shields in the form of a horse's forehead are essentially restricted to Italy.

SPAIN
The half-round "Spanish shield" is correctly named, for it appears particularly early in Spain.

HUNGARY
Here the form of the shield depends on whether the foreign influence was more German or Italian at the time.

POLAND
The form of the shields in Polish heraldry is entirely influenced by German heraldry.

RUSSIA
Russian heraldry is not indigenous; the forms of shields are copied from those in European countries.

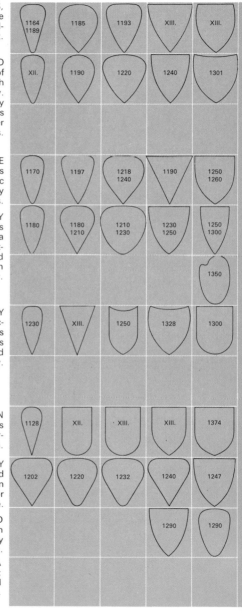

49

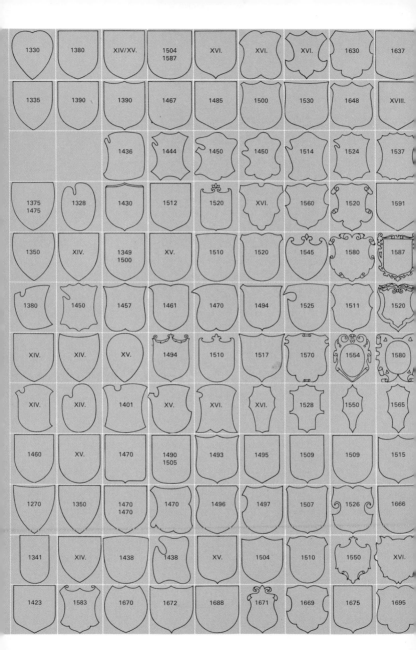

50

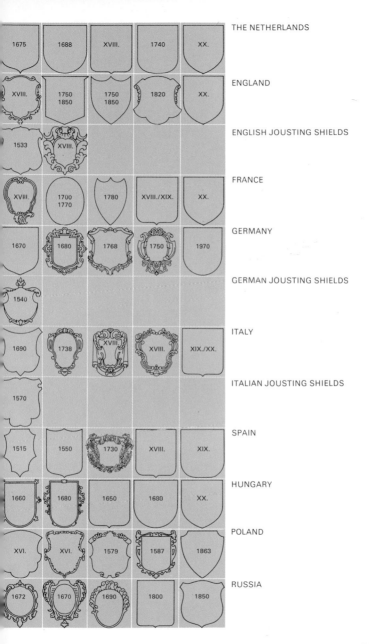

1675	1688	XVIII.	1740	XX.	THE NETHERLANDS
XVIII.	1750 1850	1750 1850	1820	XX.	ENGLAND
1533	XVIII.				ENGLISH JOUSTING SHIELDS
XVIII.	1700 1770	1780	XVIII./XIX.	XX.	FRANCE
1670	1680	1768	1750	1970	GERMANY
1540					GERMAN JOUSTING SHIELDS
1690	1738	XVIII.	XVIII.	XIX./XX.	ITALY
1570					ITALIAN JOUSTING SHIELDS
1515	1550	1730	XVIII.	XIX.	SPAIN
1660	1680	1650	1680	XX.	HUNGARY
XVI.	XVI.	1579	1587	1863	POLAND
1672	1670	1690	1800	1850	RUSSIA

51

the sign

Few words have so many meanings as "sign." This applies to all the languages of Western culture and many others. Signs can be short or long, acoustic, optical, two- or three-dimensional. Signs are the means by which men communicate with one another. In their most permanent form they are fashioned in or imprinted on some durable material and passed on to later generations.

Numbers are among the oldest signs of all. Quantities may be communicated not only by letters and figures, but also by sign language. Counting starts from graphic expression and develops via the numeral until finally we have the word which represents a number

Eskimo totem pole from Alaska with an eagle and a beaver symbolizing a family community.

The post-medieval English custom of inheriting arms as quarterings due to marriage with heraldic heiresses can lead to innumerable and repeated quarterings.

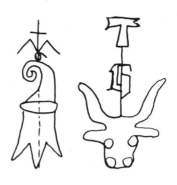

and can be expressed in letters. All scripts have arisen out of picture writing, and that includes cuneiform writing. Being rather laborious, this was, during the last millennium before Christ, completely superseded by the more flexible Phoenician-Greek-Roman alphabet. The number of writing systems is infinitely great, and even today phonetic scripts and writing in letters have not penetrated everywhere.

Writing in letters depends on general agreement as to the pronunciation of those letters. At present, there is actually a swing away from letters toward pictographs. People in every country know the wordless signs for "ladies" and "gentlemen," for "no smoking," for overtaking and no overtaking on the highway, for stop and go. A person is officially obliged to learn a large number of signs before he can drive an automobile; and half the people in developed countries drive, including the completely illiterate. The advantage of picture language and picture writing lies in the fact that knowledge of the spoken language is unnecessary, and people can find their way around in foreign sur-

roundings. But in order to make effective contact with one's fellows one also needs to know the spoken word.

Even now there are large parts of the world in which signs have yet to be replaced by writing in letters. This is particularly so in the gigantic area dominated by the Chinese.

The Teutons used letters called runes and gave them names by which they could be most unmistakably identified, rather as one says "C for Caesar" on the telephone to-

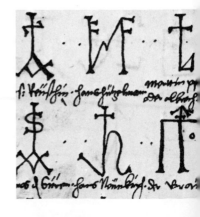

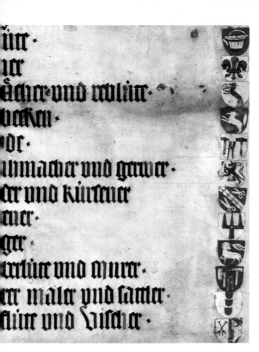

The effect of a sign depends on the associations it arouses. Graphic signs have served to designate property since time immemorial (brand sign, *above*). Watch order of the guilds of Basel with their arms, 1415 *(left)*. "Watermarks" *(far left)*: the invention of paper raised the question of how the manufacturer of the paper could identify himself on his precious product. Trading sign of a business company, Nuremberg around 1500 *(below)*.

day. Runes were also used for prophecy. Following a long period when they were of interest only to scholars, runes acquired a new and specious glory in the twentieth century, as part and parcel of delusions of grandeur based on spurious Germanic ideals. This sudden popularity was encouraged by a formal similarity between runes and "private marks," signs requiring only a few lines to distinguish one from another.

Numerous lists and surveys handed down from the Middle Ages show how whole professional groups—stonemasons, or fishermen, or merchants, and also village communities— used such signs in common. Their function was to identify the articles they produced, their tools, farm equipment, or manufactured wares, so as to avoid confusion within a particular area.

COLORS, FURS, AND DIAPERS

The colors of many very early arms are known to us only because the compilers of armorial rolls were such keen collectors. Even though it is not expressly mentioned by the earliest authors, one quickly realizes when looking at these collections that in heraldry there are as few colors as there are modern traffic signs. There are in fact six: yellow, white, red, blue, black, and sometimes green; very occasionally we also find a purple tint, a mixture of red and blue known as purpure.

The basic rules for heraldic painting stem from the function of arms as a recognition sign on the battlefield. In every coat of arms, gold or silver—

BLUE = AZURE
Planet: Jupiter.
Precious stone:
sapphire.
Symbol of: fidelity,
steadfastness.
Hatching:
horizontal lines.

ORANGE
No planet sign.
No precious stone.
Symbolism: indefinite.
Hatching:
combination of red lines
and gold dots.

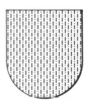

almost invariably represented by yellow and white—must appear at least once. These are the "metals," which in the classic heraldic traditions of

56

SILVER = WHITE = ARGENT
Planet: Moon.
Precious stone: pearls.
Symbol of: cleanliness,
wisdom, innocence,
chastity, joy.
Hatching: none.

ED = GULES
lanet: Mars.
recious stone: Ruby.
ymbol of: eagerness
serve one's
therland.
atching: vertical lines.

The old heralds also called the colors
after planets and precious stones.
The system of hatching as a means of
identifying colors was invented in the
late sixteenth century and became
established after 1638.

BLACK = SABLE
Planet: Saturn.
Precious stone: diamond.
Symbol of: mourning.
Hatching:
combination of the
lines for red and blue.

REEN = VERT
anet: Venus.
ecious stone: emerald.
ymbol of: freedom,
auty, joy, health, hope.
atching: diagonal
nes "in bend."

PURPLE = PURPURE
Planet: Mercury.
Precious stone:
amethyst.
Symbol of: majesty.
Hatching: diagonal
lines "in bend sinister."

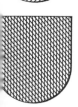

BROWN = TENNÉ
Instead of a planet,
dragon's head.
Prec. stone: hyacinth.
Symbol of: natural color.
Hatching: comb. of the
lines for red and green.

medieval chivalry were always
used alternately with the "colors." The colors in order of
frequency of their appearance
are red, blue, black, and green.
They can be used for the
ground of a shield or the coloring of a charge, but in each
case the remaining parts
should be in metal.

The rule cannot of course be
strictly applied when for one
reason or another a coat of
arms shows three different colors, as when the field is divided
into three sections, or when
the charge covers a dividing

57

ERMINE ERMINES

Before the adoption of the hatching used today to denote colors in black and white representations of coats of arms, printed outlines were used in wood or copper engraving which could then be colored in by hand. Small letters were used as a key, on or beside the area to be painted, usually the initial letters of the colors in the language of the country concerned. Black was usually printed either as a solid (with wood blocks) or as very close hatching (with copper engravings). This was later to lead to numerous mistakes, with close horizontal hatching, for example, being mistaken for blue instead of black.

line without the colors being "counterchanged."

A certain amount of tolerance is therefore called for when applying the rules of heraldry regarding color on color or metal on metal. An example is the flag of the Federal Republic of Germany. This is considered wrong in heraldic terms because black and red are next to each other, and not separated by the gold. For banners and flags, the rules of heraldry are generally relaxed.

In heraldry proper, the pattern of the material is of no significance. To add an air of luxury to the execution, the single color of a field may be patterned or "diapered," and this is not mentioned in the

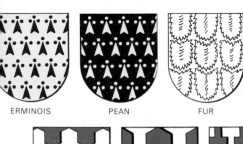

ERMINOIS · PEAN · FUR

VAIR

GROS VAIR

POTENT

VAIRY

blazon, since the pattern remains a matter for the discretion of the artist. Diapering was also used to enliven the flat surface of armorial shields. One must distinguish diapering from the "furs"—particularly ermine and vair—which are subject to strict rules.

The stylized form of ermine goes back to the time when it was fastened with a clasp or three pins whose heads were like a cloverleaf. The cleanliness of the ermine was legen-

In the Middle Ages and in early modern times, emotive values were attached to the colors, and it is interesting to note that certain color compositions are preferred or avoided by one race or another.

dary, and was expressed in the saying *Potius mori quam feodari* ("Rather die than be soiled").

Above: Tiles with the arms of Swiss families in the monastery of St. Urban in the canton of Lucerne, probably shortly after 1308.

THE BASIC ORDINARIES

The aim of all blazon is to make an unequivocal statement about the way in which the armorial shield should be arranged. It may consist of an undivided field containing one or more charges. Or it may be divided in an number of different ways.

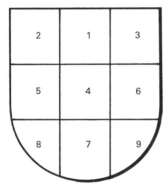

DESCRIPTION OF THE SHIELD

An armorial shield can be divided up into different areas and points, which are explained below. When the shield is divided so as to accommodate several different coats of arms, this is done by "quartering." The system of numbering shown is traditional in Continental heraldry, and the areas it delineates are named as follows: 1–3, Chief; 4–6, Fess; 7–9, Base; 2–8, Dexter; 3–9, Sinister; 1–7, Pale.

The midpoint of the line connecting 1 and 4 is known as the honor point. The center of 4 is the fess point. And the midpoint of the line connecting 4 and 7 is the nombril or navel point.

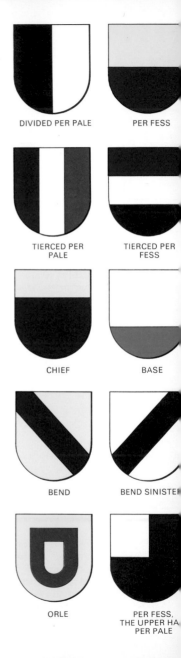

DIVIDED PER PALE

PER FESS

TIERCED PER PALE

TIERCED PER FESS

CHIEF

BASE

BEND

BEND SINISTER

ORLE

PER FESS, THE UPPER HALF PER PALE

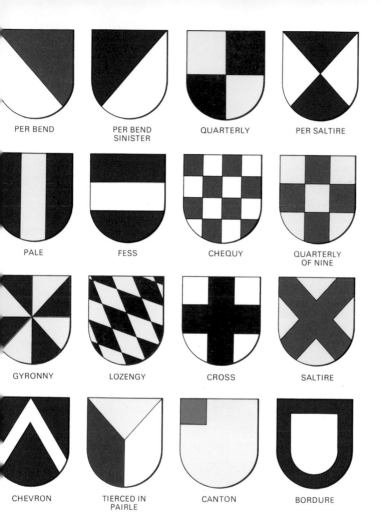

PER BEND PER BEND SINISTER QUARTERLY PER SALTIRE

PALE FESS CHEQUY QUARTERLY OF NINE

GYRONNY LOZENGY CROSS SALTIRE

CHEVRON TIERCED IN PAIRLE CANTON BORDURE

The division of colors and metals is achieved with "lines of partition." The basic divisions are those of the "honorable ordinaries," or as the French have it, *pièces honorables.*

The lines of partition can be varied in innumerable imaginative ways. The only restriction is in the rule of alternation of color and metal. The superimposition of color upon color and metal upon metal is forbidden; so in theory are their juxtaposition, but this cannot always be avoided when for instance three different sections lie adjacent to one another (see shields pp. 60–61, "tierced in pairle" and "per fess, the upper half per pale"). Most heraldic badges

Arms of Lord Baltimore consisting of the family arms of Calvert in the first and fourth quarters and of Crossland in the second and third quarters.

have conventional names, particularly the ordinaries, which are the basic charges made up of straight lines. A line dividing a shield when only two colors are used is per fess or per pale. But if three colors are used it remains a horizontal or vertical partition, with the

sequence as follows: Paly of four (Partition); two Pales (Ordinary); Paly of six (Partition); three Pales (Ordinary); Paly of eight (Partition); four Pales (Ordinary). An incalculable number of variations can be achieved with combinations of partitions and ordinaries alone. Examples are the silver pale with one black chevron in a red field of the Swiss von Erlachs and next to it the pale with three chevrons of the von Nidau family, a branch of the counts of Neufchâtel. All branches of this family have pales with three or six chevrons, the chevrons either black on a gold pale in a red field or silver on a red pale against a gold ground. This is how the cousins "differenced" their arms, including the von Badenweilers of the Black Forest. The von Erlachs, with their single chevron, were Neufchâtel vassals.

Badges that have enough space—in particular, crosses and chevrons—can be and often are accompanied by smaller elements. In French heraldry, for example, chevrons between three stars occur so frequently that they no longer serve the purpose of identification.

ENGRAILED

INVECTED

WAVY

NEBULY

INDENTED

DANCETTY

EMBATTLED

DOVETAILED

POTENTY

RAGULY

URDY

RAYONNÉ

"FIR TREE TOP SECTION"

"FIR TWIG SECTION"

"CLOVERLEAF SECTION"

Below: A sample from the so-called Redinghoven armorial in the Bavarian State Library, Munich, named after its discoverer, the archivist of Jülich-Berg, Johann Gottfried Redinghoven (d. 1704). Compiled before 1440, it contains mainly southern German arms, serving here as an example of "partitions."

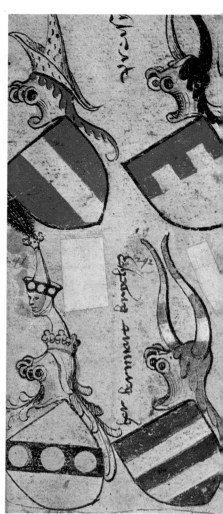

A work by a Dutchman, Jean-Baptiste Rietstap, is of inestimable value in the science of heraldry. Rietstap collected 116,000 coats of arms from the armorials available some hundred years ago and prepared them for printing with blazons in impeccable French. His *Armorial général*

appeared in Gouda in 1884. It contains an introduction of several pages of text and illustrations in which the technical expressions are carefully explained and their origin documented wherever possible. The opposite page shows one of these illustrations.

1 Chevron couped in chief
2 Chevronels
3 Chevronels disjointed
4 Bar dancetty of two
5 Three chevronels between two bendlets
6 Chevron couched sinister
7 Chevronny of four reversed
8 Two chevronels in counterpoint
9 Two chevrons interlaced, one reversed
10 Three chevronels fretted
11 Chevronny of four per pale
12 Chevronelly
13 Four chevronels palleted
14 Per chevron a crescent counter-changed
15 Tierced per pale
16 Cross between two shields in second and third cantons
17 Cross per saltire gules and azure
18 Cross surmounted by a chevron reverse
19 Cross gobony or and azure
20 Cross nebuly
21 Cross vairy
22 Cross with four knobs protruding
23 Cross fitched
24 Cross couped between four roses
25 Cross fretted between two eagles and two lions
26 Cross engrailed
27 Cross indented
28 Cross raguly
29 Cross moline
30 Cross moline fimbriated
31 Cross recercely
32 Cross fouchy
33 Cross gringoly
34 Cross fitched at all points, surmounted by a bar
35 Cross potent
36 Cross formy
37 Four almonds in saltire
38 Cross formy couped quarterly
39 Quarterly argent and gules four crosses formy counterchanged

40 "Key cross"
41 Cross of Toulouse
42 Potent couped and in chief a mullet
43 Patriarchal cross, the second bar rectangled sinister to the base
44 Cross potent repotent
45 Cross of nine besants
46 Saltire counter-compony
47 Saltire compony
48 Saltire gyronny of sixteen
49 Cross portate counter-compony
50 Two pales surmounted by a saltire counter-compony
51 Saltire engrailed
52 Saltire of nine lozenges
53 Pall
54 Pall couped pointed
55 Tierced per pairle
56 Pall reversed
57 Tierced per pairle reversed
58 Pile reversed in base
59 Per pile transposed
60 Per fess and per pile transposed or and azur, three roses gules
61 Quarterly and per pile transposed gules and argent counterchanged
62 Per pile reversed arched azure two fleurs-de-lis or and or a rose gule
63 Or a point pointed sable a fleur-de-lis or
64 Gules three bars and two points dexter and sinister argent
65 Gules a man and two points dexter and sinister charged each with a crescent
66 Per pile gules a pale argent, and or
67 Per pil arched gules and argent
68 Per fess azure and argent, a lozenge throughout counter-changed
69 Or a pile gules
70 Point pointed in point from sinister base to dexter chief

THE RULES OF BLAZON

Half of the sixty-nine volumes of the *Armorial Général* in the Bibliothèque Nationale in Paris contain illustra-

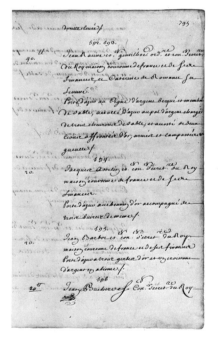

tions, and the other half the technical descriptions (or blazons as they are known in heraldic terminology). Here is a sample page.

The technical description of a coat of arms is called a "blazon," a term thought to derive from the German word *blasen*, to blow, probably referring to the stentorian tones of the herald proclaiming the armorial bearings of a person. The word was then taken into the French language, the "mother tongue" of heraldry. The method of blazoning is as follows: first the shield is described, and this also serves as a basis for the identification of unknown arms. If there are no partitions the color is stated: In…this or that object or heraldic charge, its color "declared" in adjectival form. Division creates a number of areas in the shield; if these carry their own charges they are referred to as "fields" and numbered. An interpretation of the contents of a field is given if known. Next come the helmet, mantling, and crest, if they form part of the armorial bearings, then the decorative devices, starting with those closest to the shield and moving outward.

SAN MARINO

The arms of the Republic of San Marino, legally adopted on 6 April 1862: azure, three mountain peaks vert (Monte Titano), each surmounted by a crenellated tower argent, with an ostrich feather argent, gate and windows sable. The shield is framed by a heart-shaped cartouche. The crown has three arches to symbolize sovereignty and is lined to half its height with purple. Leafy branches flank the shield and cross below it, olive on the left and oak on the right. The fluttering banderole bears the word *"Libertas"* (freedom) in letters of gold.

SAN MARINO

DENMARK

DENMARK ROYAL ARMS

The royal arms established on 5 July 1972, after the accession and the renunciation by Queen Margarethe II of her German hereditary titles, are quartered by a cross argent outlined in gules (the Danebrog cross); (1) and (4) or, nine hearts gules accompanying three lions passant azure armed and langued gules (Slesvig), (3) per fess, the lower half per pale, (a) azure, three (2, 1) crowns or (Union of Calmar), (b) azure, a ram argent standing (Faroes), (c) azure, a polar bear argent sejant (Greenland). The shield is resting on a marble base and supported by two wild men with garlands of oak leaves round their loins, armed with clubs in natural color. The whole is placed beneath a purple armorial cloak—lined with ermine and held up by tasseled golden cords—that falls from the crown of the kingdom of Denmark.

UNITED KINGDOM

Unchanged since 1837: Quartered, (1) and (4) gules, three lions or passant guardant armed and langued azure (England), (2) or with a double tressure fleury counterfleury gules, a lion gules rampant armed and langued azure (Scotland), (3) azure, a harp or with strings argent (Ireland). The shield is surmounted by a king's helmet in gold with gold and ermine mantling and the following crest: standing upon the imperial state crown of Great Britain a lion as in fields (1) and (4), but armed and langued red and wearing the imperial state crown. The shield is surrounded by the emblem of the Order of the Garter; the supporters are, on the right, a golden lion guardant, armed and langued red and wearing the imperial state crown (England), and on the left a silver unicorn with a golden crown around its neck, its mane and hooves golden, and with a gold chain. The shield rests on a compartment of grass on which are placed the floral emblems of the United Kingdom—a silver and red rose (England), a natural thistle (Scotland), and a shamrock (Ireland)—and a blue banderole edged with gold bearing the inscription *"Dieu et mon droit"* (God and my right).

UNITED KINGDOM

67

SIGNS OF DIFFERENCING
AND AUGMENTATIONS OF HONOR

One of the original guiding principles of heraldry was that a coat of arms should clearly identify a particular person while at the same time attaching some importance to the family he belonged to. This led to the creation of distinguishing signs (in French *brisures*), minor changes which did not affect the overall impression of the shield. Certain conventions for this process were developed. In many procedure of using a mark of difference for individuals is still customary, and this is done to the greatest extent in the royal family.

The system of a special mark of difference known as a "label" for each member of the family goes back to the time of Henry III (reigned 1216–1272), whose successor, as a prince, placed such a mark on the shield of England. Initially there was no particular system

The marks of difference for the second to tenth sons (crescent, mullet, martlet, annulet, fleur-de-lis, rose, cross moline, anchor, and double quatrefoil).

Right: Basically the children of a British monarch receive a silver label with three points on which certain small symbols are arranged symmetrically.

CHARLES   ANNE   ANDREW

places the crest also served as a means of distinguishing individuals and as a result their own family lines. Great Britain is the only country in the world in which the classical in the representation of this sign; however, no doubt on visual grounds, it was almost always white and overlaid with small figures. The number of points was not critical.

Two examples of marks of favor from Belgium: the lion from the state arms *(left)* and the initials of King Leopold III.

The differencing of a prince's arms extends to the supporters on whose shoulders the label appears. In the arms of a prince an ingeniously devised system of crowns of rank must also be observed, which serves to indicate the relationship of generations between the prince and the sovereign.

A distinction must be made between the marks distinguishing the different members of a particular family and marks of favor. In almost all countries, and particularly those with a monarchy, additional signs are granted to deserving people, and also communities, which are mostly de-

Right: Coat of arms of the well-known diplomat and statesman Charles-Maurice de Talleyrand-Périgord, Prince of Bénévent (1745–1838). Arms as Napoleonic prince of Bénévent, consisting of the imperial eagle in chief, and beneath it the ancestral arms and the boar of Bénévent; also the chain of the *grand aigle* of the *Légion d'honneur* and armorial drape with a prince's crown.

Below: The knights of the *Légion d'honneur* placed their cross of the order on a red honorary piece. The Napoleonic counts and barons were given a canton in their arms serving as the position for a personal emblem.

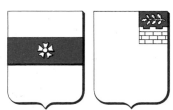

veloped from the state sign of sovereignty and appear in a chief or a canton.

HERALDIC STYLES

The arms of the kingdom of Bohemia in different styles *(from left to right):*

The oldest careful representation of the arms of Bohemia in the colors of the folding table of Lüneburg, about 1328.

Schematic drawing of the same arms from the armorial roll of Zurich (ca. 1340).

Representation in the Flemish style by the Gelre herald (ca. 1380). The lion is highly ornamental, almost grotesque.

Illustration from the armorial of Konrad Grünenberg, Constance, 1483.

Illustration from the armorial of Virgil Solis, 1555. The colors of the mantling match those of the shield. The drawing aims for maximum symmetry. The chain is that of the Order of the Golden Fleece. Whoever was king of Bohemia was at that time also a knight of that order.

Before heraldry acquired its name, signs existed which were so well known that they could serve as a means of recognition. These signs were subject to a traditional manner of representation which constituted the heraldic style. This was to become the outstanding feature of heraldry. The heraldic style refers to a type of representation which was subjected to fairly strict rules, but was quite flexible within those rules.

The strictness of these rules resulted from the necessity of recognizing a sign at some distance or at high speed—the very same necessity to which

The stylization of the lion stemmed from the desire for symmetry. In the first picture the body forms a central axis; the strongly formed tail counterbalances the extended legs.

As shields became wider the arrangements of the lion's limbs altered. The right hind leg is now held out horizontally.

In the late Gothic period it was more important to fill the available space than to have the lion upright. The axis is therefore inclined until the body is almost horizontal.

heraldry owed its being. The directness of the impression was initially provided by the contrast between light and dark colors. However, the contrasting patches of color soon proved insufficient to indicate the necessary differences, and therefore pictures had to be added which could be recognized by their silhouette.

This is where the heraldic style appears most clearly. One of its requirements is that figures should fill the available space as far as possible. The skill of the heraldic painter lies especially in his ability to strike a balance between the superimposed figure and the negative shape of the surrounding background colors, formed in part by the outline, and in part by the background patterning. The texturing of the background, technically known as

"diapering," is not normally defined in the blazon, the heraldic description, but left entirely to the artist. It offers scope for vitality, relieving the severity of the heraldic style. Magnificent designs have been produced in this way, and art historians consider these an important element in style analysis.

The solid cross developed forms which moved with the tiplication of the horizontal arms, which were linked with hierarchical status. The flat cross reached basically to the edge of the ground on which it was painted, while the solid cross, as it was fre-standing, could have highly ornamented arms.

The shape of fields available for a coat of arms can be greatly varied. Historically, however, one starts with the three-

Arms of an English lord around 1390 from the chapel seat which he received as a knight of the Order of the Garter. Typical of English arms of the period are the over-weighted helmet and crest, and the fringed mantling falling away toward the back and ending in a thick tassel.

There are two points characteristic of Polish heraldry: a) the majority of the old arms contain figures in linear form; and b) several families without any known relationship between them can bear the same arms.

style of the times and were characterized by the faceting of the arms, particularly by the broadening of the ends of the arms, which were strongly reminiscent of letters. At the same time there was a mul- cornered field which approximates the three-cornered shield of the medieval knight. The next basic form is the rectangle, sometimes long, sometimes wide, and sometimes square. The fitting of the ar-

Arms of a central European noble family. The shield is broad at the bottom to accommodate numerous charges. Narrow-bodied animals (and also men) are typical of German heraldry.

Arms of an English family, the various branches of which bear the same arms in different colors. There is no contact between the upright shield and the helmet.

In Italy the jousting shield lasted longest as a part of the full achievement of arms. It is in this country that the clearest distinction was made between a jousting shield *(targa)* and the more conventional form *(scudo)*.

morial picture or "charge" into the outline of the background may require considerable adjustment, and the most frequent figures are often distorted in one way or another for this purpose. A different kind of distortion—one of the hallmarks of the heraldic style—is the altered coloring of certain parts of an animal's body. The claws and tongue of the lion, the claws and beak of the eagle, also the antlers of the deer, and the hooves and horns of other animals may be colored differently from the rest of the body, frequently according to definite rules.

This is more strictly observed in England than elsewhere. The lions in the arms of England, and therefore also in those of Canada, are golden in a field of red, and their tongue and claws are blue; when they are freestanding, on the helmet, tongue and claws are red. The rule that color should not be placed next to color, nor metal next to metal, obviously has to be disregarded, even in England, when it becomes impossible to observe. That is the case for instance when a golden lion is placed on a field divided into red and blue. Juxtaposition of the two colors is less reprehensible than superposition, and as soon as a figure is superposed, the question of infringement of the rule no longer arises at all. The term "riddle arms" is used, generally implying an invitation to find the solution to the riddle posed by a color fault, but in this case it may be ignored.

The color rules of heraldry have been observed more or less from the beginning, for good and practical reasons. A certain relaxation set in when heraldry started to decline, around the year 1500, and presentation in natural color became more prevalent. The turn of the century around

Right: The difference between a natural flower and its heraldic representation can be considerable. Indeed, it has been doubted whether the fleur-de-lis is based on the lily at all.

The arms of a conquistador *(above)* granted by Charles I of Spain in 1546. The arms bestowed on the conquerors of South America show a poverty of invention and graphic skill which reflects the decline of Spanish heraldry, hitherto cultivated to a high degree.

Left: Arms of Pope Pius II, 1458—1464. The so-called horse-head shield is a result of striving in the Renaissance for symmetrical forms. The tiara at the top gives a more pleasing effect than the helmet and crest.

1500 altogether marked a crisis point in heraldry, for it was at that time that weapons technology ceased to play a role. The problem of how the two-dimensional heraldic style could be reconciled with

Right: Arms of the head of a Portuguese family *(chefe)* around 1500. The idea that each coat of arms had to represent a particular person persisted in Portugal beyond the end of the Middle Ages.

These shields were transferred from one armorial collection to another, with adjustments. They are shown above, after the book of the Council of Constance (1414—1418), and below in the armorial of Virgil Solis, Nuremberg 1555.

naturalistic qualities occupied no less a person than the great Albrecht Dürer. This problem emerges very clearly when one considers the image of the lion, the heraldic beast most widely portrayed. During the nineteenth century, it came more and more to resemble its cousin in the zoo, or even a shorn poodle. A return to the classic forms of the Gothic

period went hand in hand with renewed interest in "patriotic pieces." As a result, the Gothic style has come to be rather overvalued, even to this day, in all parts of the world. It should be remembered, how-

ever, that the Gothic style of one country may well differ from that of another, particularly in heraldry. This may be a matter of the choice and design of the escutcheon and its contents, but decorative accessories show it most clearly. The helmet and even more so its mantling play a major role in this—unless of course they are neglected as parts of an achievement. This neglect is to be found chiefly in the Romanic countries and had its origin in the architectonic designs of the Renaissance style which favored the use of crowns, particularly crowns of rank.

Registers not based on family names are generally arranged according to shield contents. This is the system used with the arms of every independent country in the world, as shown in the following pages.

THE CROSS

In the Christian world, the cross has unique significance as an armorial sign. It is the first common emblem under which the men of western Europe gathered, though initially, when the first Crusade was announced, the color of the cross was of no significance.

the battle at the Pons Milvius was actually meant to represent a cross, let alone the cross of Christ's passion. The soldiers of the victorious emperor were given an official description so that they could paint it on their shields. The description indicates clearly that the

Flag of the Byzantine empire, from a book on the flags of the fourteenth century, the *Conoscimiento de todos los Reinos.* This flag of the emperor of Constantinople consists of a combination of St. George's Cross (red on a white ground) with the arms of the ruling family of the Paleologues. The four charges in the corners of each of the other two crosses can be seen either as fire steles, or as the Greek letter B.

Nor do we know the exact shape of the cross which Christians had looked upon in reverence before that time.
Indeed, it cannot even be said with certainty that the famous sign of victory which the emperor Constantine followed in

sign was unknown to the soldiers. In fact, it consisted not of a cross but of two letters. One of them at least was made up of two crossed shafts, but this cross lay diagonally and was not the upright cross we know today. Nevertheless, in

The Ascension of Christ with the banner of the cross, in white and red, bestowed on him by the artist as a sign of victory.

due course the true form of the cross was incorporated in the design of the monogram of Christ. What has been estab-lished dence of this may be found in many of the coins of emperors who recognized Christianity as a state religion.

lished is that after Constan-tine's victory over Maxentius in A.D. 312, an old Roman ban-ner, the *labarum*, served as an imperial standard and the monogram of Christ was add-ed, either on the end of the staff or on the flag itself. Evi-

This painting of the school of Raphael somewhat anticipates reality, for in addition to carrying the *labarum*, the whole army is equipped with crosses on their standards.

Fifty-six types of cross in
heraldry:

1 Cross
2 Cross fillet
3 Cross per fess
4 Cross per pale
5 Cross quartered
6 Cross gyronny
7 Cross gyronny of sixteen
8 Cross faceted
9 Cross counter-compony
10 Cross fretty
11 Cross double voided
12 Cross cotised
13 Cross fimbriated
14 Saltire or St. Andrew's cross
15 Cross couped
16 Saltire couped
17 Passion cross
18 Passion cross with both bars
   the same length
19 Patriarchal cross
20 Patriarchal cross with third bar
21 Russian cross
22 Cross formy
23 Cross pattée concave
24 Cross formy couped
25 Cross potent
26 Jerusalem cross
27 Cross crosslet
28 Cross degraded
29 Cross calvary
30 Cross moline
31 Cross recercely
32 Cross moline quarter-pierced
33 Maltese cross
34 Cross fleuretty
35 Cross of any Iberian order of
   knighthood
36 Cross gringoly
37 Cross fourchy
38 Cross fitchy
39 Cross bottony
40 Cross pommy
41 "Key" cross
42 Cross of Toulouse
43 Cross barby
44 Cross formy fitchée couped
45 Cross fitchée double
46 Cross indented
47 Cross engrailed
48 Cross invected
49 Cross bretessed
50 Cross embattled-counter-
   embattled
51 Cross raguly
52 Cross raguly counter raguly
53 Cross raguly and trunked
54 Cross wavy
55 Swastika couped in saltire
56 Fylfot

78

THE UNION JACK

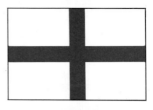

In 1606 the red cross of St. George (England) was combined with the

blue-and-white saltire of St. Andrew (Scotland) to form the first Union

Early in the fifteenth century, the cult of St. George became established in England. His arms as the patron saint of knights, a red cross on a white ground, became the national badge and also became the national flag of England, in addition to the three-lion banner of the king. The patron saint of Scotland is St. Andrew, and the instrument of his martyr-

dom, a white saltire cross on a blue ground, has been the country's emblem since at least the twelfth century.

The gradual union of the two countries, from 1603 onward, found expression in the combination of the two crosses, with St. Patrick's cross (red on a white ground) added in 1801. This is interlaced with the cross of St. Andrew.

Jack. Since 1800 and as a consequence of the establishment of the

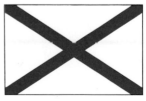

"United Kingdom of Great Britain and Ireland" the saltire *(bottom)* of St. Patrick (Ireland) was incorporated into the Union Jack.

Oldest known representation of the Danebrog in the arms of Denmark as shown in the late fourteenth century; *Gelre Armorial.*

The white cross on red has been employed consistently as the chief Danish symbol—used in variations for naval and military purposes as well—for at least 600 years.

THE DANEBROG

The Danebrog, or Dannebrog in Danish, is the national flag of Denmark. It is thought the word might mean the "Danish cloth." The cloth of this flag is red and divided into four by a white cross. In the official design, the cross is placed so close to the shaft that the corner fields are exactly square.

It is not certain how this cross came to be the national em-

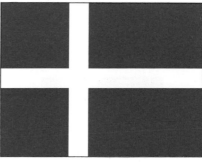

blem. Legend has it that when King Waldemar II of Denmark won his final victory over the heathen Estonians on 15 June 1219, the day was won only because the banner dropping from heaven, i.e., sent by God, turned the scales at the very moment when all seemed lost. The true reason was probably that the Pope sent a banner of the cross to be carried in a missionary campaign.

THE CROSS
IN NATIONAL COATS OF ARMS

ICELAND ▷

The shield bears the cross introduced to the flag on 1 December 1918. It is supported by the four "protectors."

◁ GREECE

The Greeks fought under the cross of Christ from 1821 onward, freeing themselves from Islamic rule. They have remained faithful to the cross.

JAMAICA ▷

In the oldest British colonial arms, five pineapples are placed on the Cross of St. George.

◁ SWITZERLAND

The cross of the Holy Roman Empire, badge of the Federation from the fourteenth century, and the arms of the Federation since 1815.

DOMINICAN REPUBLIC ▷

A trophy of flags, lances, a cross, and the Gospels superimposed on the design of the national flag.

◁ FIJI

Sugar cane, coconut palm, dove of peace, and bananas arranged around the British Cross of St. George.

GRANADA ▷

The ship of Columbus, discoverer of the island, and with it a lion (power of the nation) and the lily of the Virgin Mary in a crescent.

◁ DOMINICA

The cross stands for Discovery Sunday; the coconut palm and banana tree are fruitful, the frog is edible.

SWEDEN ▷

The narrow cross separates the more recent crown arms from the oldest lion arms of the Folkunger family.

◁ GHANA

Cantoned cross, with the national emblems (regional and central) above, and symbols of prosperity below.

GEOMETRIC PATTERNS AND ORNAMENTS

Although basic geometric patterns are limited, their possible uses are far from being exhausted even today. In the political domain, despite the general tendency to use naturalistic shapes and figures that are immediately recognizable, many state arms which incorporate geometric patterns according to valid heraldic

Right: The four armorial shields on the wooden chest enable us to place it fairly accurately as coming from Pisa in the second half of the thirteenth century.

Left: The flag of the herald of the Flemish lords of Gruthuyse consists of ordinaries (cross and saltire); from the "Livre des Tournois" of King René, fifteenth century.

norms have been created in very recent years.

Some examples are shown in the ensuing pages, beginning with a series of eight state

arms, some of which reveal the influence of the art of the British heralds.

These are followed by eight state arms based on the old heraldic method of combining several pre-existing coats of arms; our selection shows only arms whose field is divided into more than four quarterings. Such combinations can be constituted in various ways. The pattern may incorporate authentic old arms, as in the case of Liechtenstein or Canada; or heraldic-type emblems or decorations, as in the arms of Australia or Malaysia; or it may even combine diverse symbols as if they had been ac-

Erlib Bern Frei von nin huene / ris had herr Boygen gen

tual heraldic arms, as can be seen in the case of New Zealand, Tonga, the Central African Republic, or Panama. The actual "quarterly" arms (i.e., with field divided into four sections or quarterings) are arranged according to their first quarterings—the upper-left-hand section from the viewer's standpoint, called "dexter" in heraldry.

The geometrically patterned arms on the following pages conclude with four (p. 89) in which local concerns rather than heraldic rules have prevailed, and the principal element of the arms consists of initials or inscriptions.

85

GEOMETRIC PATTERNS AND ORNAMENTS IN NATIONAL COATS OF ARMS

KOREA (SOUTH) ▷
The "T'ae-guk" (yin-yang in Chinese) represents the male and female principles pertaining everywhere.

◁ HUNGARY
Discarding ancient traditions, the Hungarians only used their national colors in their armorial shield design of 1956.

MALTA ▷
In 1975, the shield divided per pale, with the George Cross, was replaced with a boat in the sun.

◁ BAHRAIN
The silver sectioned chief over a red field was based on the current national flag.

CHAD ▷
The shield, seven times divided dancetty in gold and blue, is supported by a moufflon "à manchettes" and a lion.

NIGERIA▷

The confluence of the Niger (= black) and Benue is indicated by the white pall wavy in black.

UNITY AND FAITH

ONE ZAMBIA ONE NATION

◁ZAMBIA

The Zambesi flowing in black soil; mine, zebra and corncob beneath the shield.

LIECHTENSTEIN▷

The arms of Silesia, Kuenring, Troppau, East Frisia, and Jaegerndorf, and the inescutcheon of the dynasty.

◁ MONACO

The silver and red lozengy in pale shield of the Grimaldi family is supported by two armed monks.

CENTRAL AFRICAN REPUBLIC▷

Quarterly in the national colors, the shield contains, among other elements, the black map of Africa in the inescutcheon.

◁ TONGA

"God and Tonga are my inheritance"
says the motto beneath the shield,
which is Victorian in style.

PANAMA ▷

Symbols of peace and progress surround the isthmus in the light of the
sinking sun of 3 November 1903.

◁ CANADA

Granted in 1921, the coat of arms
includes the French fleur-de-lis and the
maple leaves with the British coat of
arms.

AUSTRALIA ▷

The emblems of New South Wales, Victoria, Queensland, South and Western
Australia, and Tasmania.

◁ NEW ZEALAND

Granted in 1911, these arms combine
the Southern Cross of the national flag
with symbols of prosperity.

◁ MALAYSIA

Around the colors of the ''Federals''
Negri Sembilan, Pahang, Perak, Treng-
ganu, the emblems of the other parts.

CAPE VERDE▷

A star overlying a hoe, a cogwheel, a
book, and a motto above a seashell
between corncobs.

◁ UPPER VOLTA

The initials of the country on the
national colors. These represent the
Black, White, and Red Volta rivers.

AFGHANISTAN▷

Retaining the circlet of wheat ears, the
people's republic has replaced the
mosque with the word ''people.''

◁ TOGO

Two young lions defend the flagged
shield bearing the initials for ''Répub-
lique Togolaise.''

THE LION

The *Physiologus* (the second-century B.C. source book for all the medieval bestiaries) has many astonishing things to say about lions. According to it, Jacob, the father of the tribe of Israel, named his son Judah the lion cub, which is a kind of prophecy, for thousands of years later we find current the saying *Vicit leo ex tribu Juda* ("The lion of the tribe of Judah has triumphed").

Various characteristics are attributed to the lion, distinguishing it from all other animals. According to the *Physiologus* the cubs came dead into the world, and after three days the father appears and breathes on them and thus they are woken and brought to life.

The lion is the most frequently used of all heraldic beasts. So often is it used that there is a French saying: *Qui n'a pas d'armes porte un lion* ("He who has no arms bears a lion"). The appearance of the lion as an armorial beast in a particular country by no means indicates that it forms part of the native fauna. Thus its popularity cannot come from direct acquaintance, but from the significance attributed to it. It stands as a symbol of strength and agility. In fables it is described as "noble": the king of the beasts. It may also be used as a symbol for Christ.

The lion's authority over animals does not include the birds, however, for none may command them. This antagonism between the two animal kingdoms is paralleled by an heraldic antagonism which makes the eagle the symbol of imperial power and the lion of royal sovereignty. There must have been a strong underlying sense of this antagonism in the Middle Ages, for in the heroic poem by Heinrich von Veldeke based on the story of Aeneas, the bearer of the arms of a lion is set against the bearer of the arms of an eagle. If one takes the latter to be the historical and geographical forerunner of the Holy Roman emperor, then the bearer of the lion represents the unruly feudal lords, to whom the emperor had to make more and more concessions, particularly to the powerful Duke of Bavaria and Saxony, Henry the Lion (1129–1195) of the house of Guelph. Duke Henry did not bear arms in the technical sense, but he used a naturalistic picture of a lion as a seal and erected a monumental and lifelike bronze lion outside his castle of Dankwarderode in

The oldest known seal of Richard I apparently bore only two lions. But from about 1195 on his device began to consist of three, as in the banner above. The lions continue to this day to be the heraldic emblem of England.

Brunswick. It was left to his descendants to adopt a formal coat of arms, with two lions passant, which was derived from the arms of England, which had three such lions. Henry referred to himself in Latin as *Henricus Leo,* but permitted two translations to be used in German, *Heinrich der Löwe* (Henry the Lion) and *Heinrich Welf* (Guelph). *Welf* or *Welp* was a young beast of prey, cognate with the word for a young dog, whelp, which is used in English today.

In a society which prized the noble but fierce behavior which was the essence of knightly virtues, the lion, the king of the beasts, was a highly appropriate animal for a coat of arms. As Thomasin von Zerklaere relates in his long didactic poem *Der Wälsche Gast (The Foreign Guest),* the beast was habitually accompanied by a dog, which had to bear the blows meant for the lion when the latter had done wrong. And, the author tells us, a lord should do likewise. In heraldry the lion is normally portrayed in a highly stylized fashion. The most common position is termed "rampant" (from the Latin *rapere,* to rob), that is, rearing up, with its forepaws in the air. When the

91

Example of the stylization of the heraldic lion: the lion of Bohemia, with its characteristic double tail. Lion shield from the grave of King Ottokar I; Prague, fourteenth century.

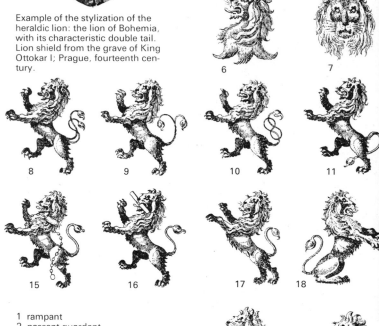

1 rampant
2 passant guardant
3 passant
4 rampant guardant
5 rampant reguardant
6 erased head

7 head guardant
8 double-queued
9 queue fourchy
10 queue nowed
11 cowed
12 truncated at snout and claws
13 defaced

14 dismembered
15 with a collar and chain
16 retrieving
17 salient
18 sejant, turned to sinister
19 sejant
20 sejan with pierced tail

21 sejant, the right forepaw raised
22 passant reguardant
23 demi lion, passant
24 trunk, couped
25 demi lion issuant, with crown around neck

26 demi lion issuant reguardant with a crenelated crown
27 sejant
28 sejant with front paws raised
29 two lions counter passant
30 two lions turned away from one another
31 two lions respectant

32 standing
33 standing with outstretched tail
34 couchant
35 sleeping

36 bicorporate
37 tricorporate
38 bicapitated
39 counter-sejant
40 winged, standing
41 St. Mark's lion sejant
42 St. Mark's lion from the Ionian islands
43 sea lion with raised tail
44 sea lion with lowered tail, standing
45 sea lion with lowered tail, upright
46 sea lion with a dragon's tail
47 chimera

Section from a Venetian flag with the lion of St. Mark standing half on land, half on water.

blazon does not specifically mention a position, the lion may be assumed to be rampant. If he is in a different position, other terminology must be used, referring to the position of his head and limbs. An early heraldic convention found in medieval blazons uses the distinction between a lion and a leopard previously employed by the ancient Greeks. In antiquity, the lion, having a heavy mane, was generally shown in profile, while the leopard, having less hair, was shown looking toward the observer. A lion looking toward the observer therefore came to be given the name of the animal usually shown in that pose. Some of the possible combinations are as follows. The current Eng-

94

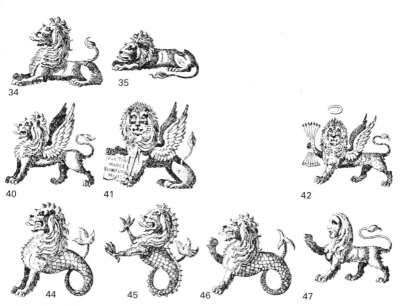

lish heraldic terms are followed by the Old French terminology.

For a lion with both forepaws raised: a lion rampant—*lion rampant.*

For a lion walking along with one forepaw raised and looking at the observer: lion passant guardant—*léopard.*

For a lion walking along and looking to the front: lion passant—*lion léopardé.*

For a lion with both forepaws raised and looking at the observer: lion rampant guardant—*léopard lionné.*

Note that the *léopard* can be recognized by the fact that it is always looking at the observer; it is always "guardant."

Burgundian embroidery showing a stylized version of the emblem of the Order of the Golden Fleece—a flint-stone striking fire.

But these distinctions are only the beginning. Any armorial figure may be painted in any of the six heraldic colors, and the lion naturally offers the most examples. It may even be patterned—with stripes running across or obliquely, checkered, or indeed per saltire. Animals can be shown holding anything capable of being held, usually in the right forepaw. Naturally in the case of a lion this is often a weapon—in the arms of the Grand Duchy of Hessen a sword, with a bundle of arrows added in the Netherlands—or the attribute of a saint, such as the axe of St. Olaf of Norway. Alternatively it may be a peaceful subject, such as the pear twig of Pope Sixtus V. This applies to any animal, but tends to be most common with the lion. When a lion has wings it nearly always relates to St. Mark, the patron saint of Venice.

Six pages from the *Armorial Equestre de la Toison d'or et de l'Europe,* early fifteenth century; Bibliothèque de l'Arsenal. Paris. The knights are, from left to right and top to bottom: the duke of Geldern, kings of Scotland and England, the dukes of Normandy and Luxembourg, and the king of Portugal.

Page 101:
Spectators of the *Joyeuse Entrée* ("joyful entry") of Mary of York into Bruges on 2 July 1468 as the wife of Duke Charles the Bold were reminded of the magnificent tableau presented to them at the Prinsenhof by this print by the Master W. A. The large lions became the ancestors of numerous supporters.

In. de. fens.

Me nemo impune l

THE LION IN NATIONAL COATS OF ARMS

NORWAY ▷

Since about 1280, the lion in the arms of Norway carries ahead of him an axe, the attribute of St. Olaf.

◁ BELGIUM

In 1830, the arms of the former dukedom of Brabant became the official arms of the newly founded kingdom.

FINLAND ▷

Armed with a west European mailed sword arm, the lion is treading a sword with a curved blade into the ground.

◁ CZECHOSLOVAK SOCIALIST REPUBLIC

On the Hussite shield, the lion of Bohemia is wearing the Slovak shield with the flames of liberty on its breast.

SRI LANKA ▷

The sword-bearing lion from the banner of the king of Kandy, deposed in 1815, was revived in 1948.

◁ NETHERLANDS

Surrounded with "shingles," the lion of Nassau bears the sword and arrows of the former States General.

IRAN ▷

The combination of a lion and the sun, an astrological image, goes back to the thirteenth century.

◁ LUXEMBOURG

The red lion on a background of white and blue stripes—the arms of Luxembourg for as long as there have been arms.

DENMARK ▷

Three lions accompanied by red hearts have been the arms of Denmark from the twelfth century.

◁ BULGARIA

The country was freed from the Turks under the lion, and the lion has survived every upheaval.

GREAT BRITAIN ▷

The shield is quartered, with the historic arms of England (twice), Scotland, and Ireland.

सत्यमेव जयते

◁ INDIA

The three lions are the capital of the column erected at Sarnath by the emperor Ashoka (272—222 B.C.).

BURUNDI ▷

The lion's head and lance were the insignia of Burundi when it was still a Belgian protectorate.

◁ SENEGAL

In 1965 the Senegal River was added to the design of the first state seal, the lion, baobab tree, and star.

ZAIRE ▷

A leopard's head above arrow and speer, with a palm frond, elephant's tusk, and the motto.

100

HERALDIC BEASTS

The roots of the pictorial language of heraldry stretch far back into pre-Christian times. The imaginary world of the creators of arms was strongly influenced by the representations of the animal world contained in the so-called bestiaries. These were books of nature middle of the second century B.C.

The lion of St. Mark should not be confused with a griffin, a fabulous beast whose upper body is that of an eagle and the lower part with the hind legs that of a lion. The griffin is shown iridescent in changing

lore which attempted to describe both biological and inanimate subjects, especially with the aim of drawing moral conclusions from them. All bestiaries go back to one original source, the so-called *Physiologus* ("one versed in natural history"), a manuscript which may have originated in Alexandria in the colors, as a symbol of luxury and its opposite, restraint. For this reason it became the emblem of a medieval order, the Tankard Order of the kingdom of Aragon. Because of this symbolism, it finally became the supporter of the arms of the Germanic Holy Roman emperor.

Who does not know the sym-

Roy de Barbaro

Early English armorials were full of stylized monsters such as the wingless wyverns ascribed to the king of Barbary.

The basilisk rarely appears as an armorial charge, except in the arms of Basel where it serves as a supporter, either singly or in pairs, for the shield bearing the "crook of Basel" *(above)*. Here it is an obvious example of canting arms.

Above left: Among the strange creatures included in the *Physiologus* is the basilisk, a gigantic bird with a swan's neck and a snake's tail. The head is that of a hen.

bol of self-abnegatory parental love, the pelican, or the phoenix rising from the ashes? But in heraldry other beasts too are perpetuated. There is the stag which drowns its enemy, the snake, in its lair and therefore appears as an armorial beast with its prey in its mouth. And the fox, of whom it is said that it feigns death in front of the birds it is going to eat.

Many fabulous creatures have become armorial beasts, and particularly supporters and badges. As the zoologists have borrowed names from the bestiaries for newly discovered types of animals, we must now make a distinction between heraldic and natural antelopes, panthers, and other exotic beasts. This becomes all the more important as the native fauna of distant countries find an increasingly important place in their heraldry.

One undisputedly mythical beast is the unicorn. In heraldry the unicorn usually has the body of a light horse, the tail of a lion, and the legs of an antelope. Its head is distinguished by the single horn and the short beard. The story that it can only be caught with the help of a virgin had a special appeal for artists. It has made

103

Phonetic associations with the word "bear" or its equivalent in other languages are quite common. There are also other reasons for the popularity of the bear. Its docility is recorded in all kinds of legends, and many a saint has made friends with a bear.

the unicorn a symbol of Christ which may be interpreted in various ways.

Pegasus, the winged horse, was introduced into heraldry with the inception of humanism. It occurs mainly in the arms of intellectuals who also count themselves poets.

Several other "kings of the animals" came from the real world of nature: first and foremost the bull and in dense forests the bear, followed by the wolf. Four-legged beasts also make very good punning or "canting" charges. In the German-speaking countries, a man with *Schwein* or *Eber* in his name inevitably chose the wild boar (Eber) for his badge. Canting arms have always been popular. The dog is easily distinguishable from a wolf or a fox, for being a domestic animal it is given a collar.

There are innumerable other examples in canting arms of animals adopted directly for their names without recourse to natural histories. There is the aurochs head of Uri, the

Seal of Queen Mary Stuart of Scotland (1542–1587).

elephant of Helfenstein (a play on *Elfenbein,* the German word for ivory). There are numerous German names which, containing the syllable *"herz,"* show a deer *(Hirsch)* or a deer's antlers in their arms. Horses on coats of arms often refer back to preheraldic symbols, an example being the horse of Lower Saxony.

NIGER▷

The sun shines upon the buffalo head and on three Tuareg weapons: lance, swords, and millet twigs.

◁VENEZUELA

The untamed white horse symbolizes freedom, the number of ears in the sheaf is that of the provinces of the country.

NAMIBIA (South West Africa)▷

Heads of a Karakul ram and African bull, with diamonds and miners' hammers (1962).

◁FAEROES

The ram, traced back to the fourteenth century, relates to the name of the country, ''sheep's isle.''

◁ PERU

The Incas believed they had dominion over three kingdoms of nature: animals (llamas), plants (Peruvian bark), and minerals.

LESOTHO ▷

The crocodile in the Bantu shield on Mount Thaba Nasiu is the tribal sign of the royal family.

◁ GUINEA

The Democratic Party used this symbol of strength before independence was achieved.

BHUTAN ▷

The name of the country, Druk-yul, means dragon country; in East Asia, the dragon is a symbol of good fortune.

◁ IVORY COAST

The elephant's head stands for the name of the country as well as the strength of the Democratic Party.

THE HUMAN FIGURE

There can be many motives for the decoration of a coat of arms, tasteful or no, with human figures or parts of the body.

Heads need not always be those of defeated enemies, as in the present-day arms of Sar-

The original arms of the kingdom of Aragon consisted of the Christian cross, through the power of which four Moorish princes had been defeated.

Right: Humorous medieval variation of a puppet figure conjuring small doubles of himself out of his pockets.

dinia, which are actually those of Aragon. The head of one's chosen lady made a more attractive subject.

No scruples were felt in exaggerating racial characteristics. Whether a lady, a moor, a saint, or some other figure,

European heraldry—not only German but also Dutch and Italian—particularly favored the human figure as a crest. Parts of the body predominated on shields.

Human figures are very frequently used as supporters.

THE HUMAN FIGURE IN
NATIONAL COATS OF ARMS

ARGENTINA ▷

Two "safe hands" hold the Phrygian cap, the Jacobite symbol of freedom, over the national colors.

◁ SOUTH AFRICA

In the first quarter of the shield Spes (hope) is represented, for Cape Province, followed by the other three provinces.

DJIBOUTI ▷

Two arms of natives threateningly hold daggers next to a native shield lying on a lance.

◁ MONGOLIA

In these arms, created in 1940 and simplified in 1960, an arat (worker) is riding toward a radiant future.

ST. VINCENT ▷

Two priestesses making a sacrifice to peace on an antique altar, arms formally granted in 1912.

109

THE EAGLE
AND OTHER WINGED
ANIMALS

In the real life of birds, too, there is a hierarchy based on physical strength. Small wonder, then, that the eagle and related species are the most widely used symbols for God and heaven. Unlike the lion, the next popular armorial beast, birds of prey occur in every geographical region, so that these sovereign creatures show a reasonable resemblance to nature even when greatly stylized.

The symbolic distinction between eagle, falcon, and hawk has an old tradition which goes back into prehistory. The Hittites used the double eagle as an emblem of sovereignty; the ancient Egyptians provided their kings with ornaments shaped like hawks and falcons which have a distinctly heraldic flavor to them. The German imperial eagle goes back directly to the ancient Romans. After his coronation in the year 800, the Emperor Charlemagne erected an im-

perial eagle on his palace at Aix-la-Chapelle. His successors "heraldicized" it so thoroughly that it has remained the emblem of Germany to this day. A hiatus arose with the view, held quite generally from the thirteenth century, but made official only by the

Emperor Sigismund in 1401, that the eagle of the emperor should have two heads, that of the future emperor only one. Following Napoleon's appearance in central Europe, the double eagle lost something of its impact, but it was not alto-

The minnesinger Reinmar of Zweter (now Zeutern in north Baden, Germany) formed the wing bones of his armorial eagle into a second and a third head.

Below left: Two town arms based on the German imperial eagle: the town of Wimpfen, with a Key; Schongau, with the Bavarian lozengy shield.

Below: The number of the United States has always been expressed by the number of stars on the American flag. Since the origin of this device is still the subject of speculation, it may be worth mentioning that this system was customary on military banners as early as the time of the Thirty Years' War (1618–1648).

gether played out. A clever move on the part of the German Roman Emperor Francis II saved it from extinction. As a symbol of imperial greatness, it was declared the arms of the Austrian empire which was rising from the ruins of the German Roman empire. As

halos around its heads. It only received halos again in 1934 when Dollfuss suppressed the word "republic" in Austria and changed the country into a "federal state" which had to ally itself with the Third Reich in 1938. The latter had a single-headed Roman eagle

Francis was emperor twice over, being both "elected Roman emperor" and "hereditary emperor of Austria," an Austrian eagle was laid on the breast of the "Roman" double eagle. But the latter, representing a worldly title, had no

distorted in a half-heraldic, half-ancient-Roman manner. The single-headed imperial eagle has lasted until today in those towns which were able to retain or regain their status as "imperial towns" in the face of increasing external sovereign-

111

One of the most impressive examples of high medieval heraldic art is the shield from the church of the Virgin Mary at Valeria near Sion in the canton of Valais, Switzerland. It proved to be the arms of one of the lines of the baronial house of Raron (Rarogne in French). It is interesting chiefly for its excellent state of preservation.

The eagle is stylized in a symmetrical manner, except for the head.

Below: Arms prepared in 1483 for the German would-be reconquest of Jerusalem. They consisted of the imperial eagle with three heads instead of two.

ty. Thus certain towns bear the same arms as the German Federal Republic. Other former imperial towns added a further sign to the eagle, usually a small shield on the breast. After many gener-

such, even after 1648, when Switzerland separated from the empire completely.

In many museums one finds glass goblets with "Quarterni-

ations of armed struggle, the Swiss gained their freedom from the empire. But the double eagle long remained a symbol of independence as

on eagles" painted on them, on each of whose pinions ranks of the empire are represented by four small shields. Thus there are four counts, four

113

The crane is a form of canting arms; the French for crane is *grue* and it is the symbol of the Gruyère region, famous for its cheeses.

landgraves, four margraves, four burgraves, and so on right down to the peasants. It is interesting that in Cologne, the "Kölsche Bur" (peasant of Cologne) still survives in the traditional carnival.

The phoenix *(below)* is differentiated from the eagle by the crest of feathers, shown here on a fifteenth-century English standard.

The eagle, a classical example of heraldry's passion for symmetry, has also been used by armorial artists in more natural forms. The eagle that symbolizes the house of Hohenzollern's refusal to yield to the Sun King soars above a landscape, the sun being the attribute that identifies the bird as an eagle. In free graphic forms (e. g., on deeds of title) even the Russian and Austrian double eagles were represented as fly-

Unlike the flat, two-dimensional shield, crests can be thought of in three dimensions and eagles can be represented more realistically, especially in their function as birds of prey.

ing in air like ordinary birds. Evidence of identity may also be provided by the smaller creatures that only the eagle is capable of killing. But not every bird of prey necessarily represents an eagle. For example, a bird with a hood over its head and ringed legs is clearly a falcon. Some birds of the eagle type turn out to be canting arms once their local name is known; a striking

example is the Saker falcon (local name: *Stocker*) in the arms of the Stocker family of Schaffhausen. An eagle-like

bird tearing its breast open is in fact a pelican feeding its young in the legendary fashion. Unlike its natural counterpart, the heraldic pelican has no bill pouch.

The strong stylization which is found in the figure of the eagle can also be applied to other winged creatures. Insects, with closed or more often with outspread wings, can have a specially decorative effect. Napoleon I made extensive use of this even when in exile on Elba.

The symbolism of the *grallatores* or long-legged wading birds is quite specific. They are identifiable by subsidiary signs. The ostrich swallows all kinds of indigestible things both in fiction and in reality. This is made clear in heraldry by the addition of some object made of iron. The crane is usually shown with a stone in its raised claw, which would wake a sleeping sentry if it fell.

115

After long wandering, the original Aztecs found the home promised by their gods under the eagle and cactus omen in the middle of a great lake. The traditional theme is interpreted in a sixteenth-century painting.

THE EAGLE
AND OTHER WINGED ANIMALS IN NATIONAL COATS OF ARMS

ALBANIA ▷

The double eagle from the family arms of the national hero Skanderbeg Kastriota has survived from the beginning.

◁ GERMANY, FEDERAL REPUBLIC

The eagle of the German emperors of the Middle Ages became the arms of the German empire in 1919, and later of the Federal Republic.

THAILAND ▷

The Garuda, the mount of Vishnu, replaced the popular white elephant in about 1910.

◁ POLAND

The Polish eagle goes back to 1222. The People's Republic has retained it without the crown.

◁ EGYPT, LIBYA, SYRIA

The Falcon of the Kuraish line of the Prophet continues to be the emblem shared since 1 January 1972.

IRAQ ▷

Following the dissolution of the Federation of Arab Republics, Iraq continued to use the eagle of Saladin.

◁ SUDAN

A secretary bird with the native shield and the motto ''Victory is ours.''

YEMEN (North) ▷

The shield worn by the eagle shows the world-famous Mariba Dam; above it, a moccha coffee shrub.

◁ AUSTRIA

In 1918 the Babenberg eagle was given the mural crown, hammer, and sickle with the shield worn on the breast; the chains followed only in 1945.

118

UNITED STATES OF AMERICA ▷

A variant of the flag on the breast of the bald eagle chosen in 1782 and later given the name "whitehead."

◁ UNITED ARAB EMIRATE

Eight links of a chain around the typical sailing ship, a dhow, on the breast of the popular hunting falcon.

SPAIN ▷

The year 1938 brought the revival of the emblems of the Catholic kings, the St. John's eagle, yoke, and arrows.

◁ INDONESIA

The Garuda bird bears a breast shield with symbols of the five principles on which politics should be based.

BHINNEKA TUNGGAL IKA

YEMEN (South) ▷

On the breast of the Saladin eagle lies a shield divided in the national colors of 1967.

PAPUA NEW GUINEA ▷

The National Emblem introduced in
1971 consists of a bird of paradise on a
Kundu drum and ornamental spear.

◁ MEXICO

According to legend, the city of Mexico
stands on the site where an eagle killed
a snake on a cactus.

MALI ▷

A condor with talons armed hovers
above the buildings of Gao in the old
kingdom of Sudan; the sun illuminates
weapons.

◁ JORDAN

The eagle, in the black of the Prophet
and on a blue globe, was designed by
King Abdullah in 1921.

CYPRUS ▷

The white dove with the olive branch in
its beak carries its deceptive message
of peace since 1960.

120

◁ KIRIBATI

The arms granted to the former Gilbert and Ellice Islands in 1937, with the frigate bird, continue to be valid.

GUYANA ▷

Arms granted in 1966. A Canje pheasant combined in this design with wavy lines and a Victoria Regia plant.

◁ KENYA

The cock of the Kenya African National Union decorates a Massai shield in the national colors, on Mount Kenya.

GUATEMALA ▷

The quezal, a colibri unable to survive in captivity, proclaims the date of independence.

◁ EQUATORIAL GUINEA

With the changes in the constitution, a cock above various tools took the place of the mangrove tree.

THE PLANT WORLD

The plants and flowers shown in the selection of Japanese *mon* are:

Chrysanthemum

Carnation

There are only two heraldic flowers in the proper sense of the word: the lily and the rose. The lily, far more than the rose, is subject to strong heraldic stylization, probably be-

Plum blossom

Chinese flower

Three mallow leaves in a wreath of wisteria

Trefoil with pendant wisteria branch pointing upward, and a butterfly

cause it is depicted in a form that greatly differs from its natural original. The fleur-de-lis as symbol of the Virgin Mary was the chief emblem of

Chrysanthemum flowers with three leaves

the kings of France. The heraldic rose takes its basis from the dog rose and hence has five petals. Rose-shaped devices

The motif of a flower seen from above is by no means restricted to the rose; one finds it in Japanese family signs or

Above: In Great Britain, floral emblems play an extremely important part among near-heraldic designs. The Wars of the Roses ended with the white and red roses of the houses of York and Lancaster being combined in a single rose of two colors, the Tudor rose. The thistle is the emblem of Scotland, the shamrock that of Ireland.

The fourteenth-century banner of Florence *(right)* bears a distinctive symbol—the fleur-de-lis—perhaps best known as the royal emblem of France. It is a traditional symbol of the Virgin Mary. While we can catalogue its modern uses, the origin of the fleur-de-lis is obscure.

Far left: The king of France on horseback; from the "Armorial Equestre de la Toison d'or et de l'Europe," early fourteenth century.

with more petals or fewer are also to be found. Correctly speaking these should be referred to as four-petaled, six-petaled, and so on.

mon, especially since these are constructed almost invariably on the basis of a circle. Flowers are rendered with the stamens in the center or also with foli-

123

The composition of the thousands of flags in existence around the world —such as those of Swiss communities—depends on distinctive symbols. While each has a meaning and history behind it, these symbols may as well simply be appreciated for their beauty. Note the abundance of plant motifs.

age and in profile. Leafy branches may be bent to form a circle.

The British custom of using as badges not only flowers but also plants (e.g., the Welsh leek) has spread throughout the English-speaking world, where national or provincial plants often have legal status as heraldic badges.

Out of the great variety of plants and flowers, in the classical period of heraldry only those were chosen as armorial charges which could be heraldically stylized.

Leaves are more frequent in heraldry than flowers, especially those with profiles. Trees, when properly stylized, are shown with just a few branches bearing characteristic leaves or fruit.

Ears, and particularly sheaves, of corn are among the earliest armorial charges of specially fertile regions.

Less aristocratic plants are also chosen, but usually only to provide canting arms.

THE PLANT WORLD
IN NATIONAL COATS OF ARMS

PAKISTAN▷

Cotton, tea, wheat, and jute with narcissi are presented in the colors of Islam, green and white.

◁JAPAN

The chrysanthemum, actually the *mon* of the imperial family, also is of course *Paulownia imperialis*.

BARBADOS▷

The island owes its name to the "bearded figtree"; above this are placed two Red Pride of Barbados flowers.

◁ST. LUCIA

Sugar canes, roses, and lilies were in a black field in 1939 (original grant), in a gold one in 1970, and are now in a green one.

BANGLADESH▷

Padi shoots surrounding a water lily (shapla flower); above this four stars and a jute plant.

SAUDI ARABIA▷
The combination of a date palm and
crossed curved swords has taken shape
gradually.

◁LEBANON
The cedar of Lebanon, almost extinct in
nature, has been the emblem of this
country for centuries.

MALDIVE ISLANDS▷
The "thousand island" state stresses
its Islamic tradition, in addition to the
palm tree and flags.

◁SÃO TOMÉ AND PRINCIPE
Products of the coconut palm support
the economy of the two islands. Motto:
Unity, decency, work.

HAITI▷
The palmetto has been regarded as the
deep-rooted tree of freedom for the
Negro peoples since 1802; weapons
are placed around it.

127

HEAVENLY BODIES

From oldest times, men have believed that all life is governed by a star. The heavenly bodies have appeared in symbolism from the dawn of time,

Quite a number of ruling families have claimed descent from the sun. The tremendous power of the sun is expressed by straight rays alternating

The banner of Jacques de Luxembourg, the Burgundian governor of Douai, which was lost to the Swiss in 1486. His family was related by marriage to the southern French dynasty which ruled from Les Baux. The proud lords of Les Baux compared themselves with the sun and bore the latter in their arms.

partly as objects of worship, partly as simple occupants of the heavens. Constellations of the stars are rare in early heraldry. In modern arms and flags of states, however, they appear quite frequently.

with flaming rays. The sun is also to be regarded as a symbol of freedom and hope for a better future, especially when only the upper half is to be seen.

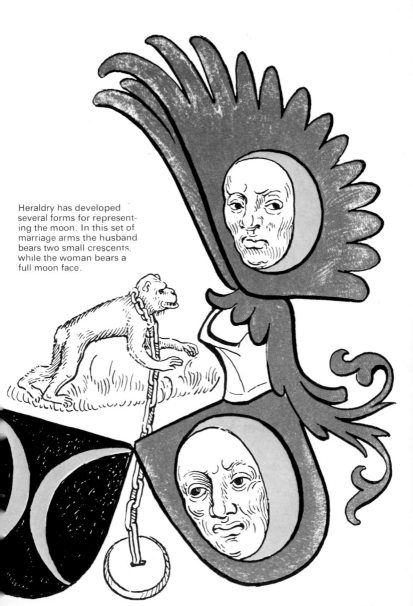

Heraldry has developed several forms for representing the moon. In this set of marriage arms the husband bears two small crescents, while the woman bears a full moon face.

129

In the arms of Morocco, on the other hand, the sun is setting, since in the native language of the country Morocco is called the *Maghreb*, that is, the West. For Ecuador the sun serves as an indicator of date, when linked with the astrological signs for the months of March to June 1845. A similar but purely naturalistic use is that of the "dawn" of revolution in Panama, which led to the establishment of a republic.

One must also regard as sun's rays the rays of light radiating from the caps which are a symbol of freedom of some Central American states.

The sun and the moon are given equal weight in the arms of Nepal, signifying that the kingdom will last as long as these heavenly bodies remain in the sky. When the Republic of Ceylon declared Sri Lanka to be its sole internationally valid name, it enriched its arms with religious symbols which included the sun and the moon. Such attitudes, based on astrological consider ations, do not appear in classical heraldry but probably form the basis of the Iranian sign of royalty, the sun in the constellation of Leo.

In the late fifteenth century, Swiss soldiers captured as booty many flags carried by Burgundian troops, including the one shown here. Its shape almost seems to have been designed especially for the sunburst design it displays.

130

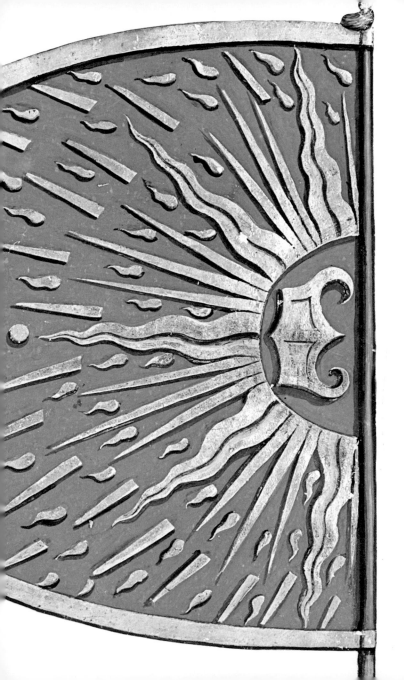

Variations of the Sun Disk flag appeared on the Shogun's warship in the seventeenth century. Farthest east of any major nation, Japan's very name, which means Source of the Sun, suggested an appropriate symbol centuries before a national flag was developed and made official.

The heavenly bodies occur more frequently in signs of royalty and sovereignty than in family arms. The moon, however, appears in non Islamic as well as Islamic lands as a favorite motif in family arms and communal heraldry as well. The waxing moon appears as a simple crescent, or with a human face in the sickle. It is often unequivocally a symbol of veneration of the Virgin Mary, with the queen of heaven represented on a horizontal crescent moon. In a blazon, the position of the moon must always be accurately stated.

Stars, either in groups or singly, appear often in arms and on flags. A star also tends to be the first choice for a mark of difference representing the sphere of heavenly bodies. Nations differ in the number of points they prefer, central Europeans giving their stars six points, Latins five.

132

THE HEAVENLY BODIES
IN NATIONAL COATS OF ARMS

MALAWI▷

The waves of Lake Njassa unite with the British lion and the sun of a new tomorrow.

◁CHINA (Taiwan)

The "white sun in a blue sky," the national coat of arms since 1928, has been the symbol for China renewed since 1895.

COMORO ISLANDS▷

Having been re-named as a federal republic, the national emblem consists of four stars for the four islands.

◁PHILIPPINES

The eight sunrays represent the provinces involved in the rising of 1896; eagle and lion, the former rulers.

TURKEY▷

From time immemorial, star and crescent have been the emblem of Islam and especially for Turkey.

◁ ALGERIA

Star and crescent, both red as for Tunisia, in a field in the colors of Islam, placed under Fatima's hand of good fortune.

DUTCH ANTILLES ▷

These arms were granted by the Queen of the Netherlands in 1964. The six stars represent the six islands.

◁ MAURETANIA

As an Islamic republic, Mauretania also has the star and crescent, and with it a palm tree and millet plants.

SINGAPORE ▷

The five stars are interpreted as symbols for democracy, peace, progress, law, and quality.

◁ CHINA (People's Republic)

The five stars from the flag shining above Mount Tien an Men and a cogwheel between rice and corn.

134

BENIN ▷

The red star on a green background dates from the name change from Dahomey to the People's Republic of Benin.

◁ WESTERN SAMOA

The Southern Cross has been placed over the U. N. emblem; beneath it is a coconut palm in the ocean (1962).

CHILE ▷

A husmu and a condor support the shield which is divided in blue and red, with one star, a variation on the flag.

◁ SOMALIA

The armorial shield shows the same design as the flag. It is pale blue, to commemorate U. N. trusteeship.

PARAGUAY ▷

The single star is said to have appeared in the flags of the rising, in about 1811; it was made official in 1842.

135

VIET-NAM▷
The yellow star from the flag was in
1956 placed above a cogwheel
between two yellow sheaves of rice.

◁GUINEA-BISSAU
The banderole bearing the motto
"Unity, Fight, Progress" winds around
a seashell.

MOROCCO▷
The green Solomon's seal from the flag
established in 1915 is shown against
the background of the Atlas Mountains.

◁ITALY
The industrious (cogwheel) nation (star)
enjoys the blessing of peace (olive
branch) and strength (oak).

BRAZIL▷
The large star in the national colors
bears the Southern Cross since 1889,
surrounded by tobacco and coffee.

136

◁ SAN MARINO

The topography of this small republic is reflected in the towers surmounted by ostrich feathers.

HONDURAS ▷

Since 1825, above a landscape with mine works, an oval containing a rainbow arching above the sun and a volcano.

◁ KOREA (north)

According to Article 147 of the constitution, the coat of arms has a hydroelectric power station beneath the red star.

ROMANIA ▷

The 1965 constitution brought a change of name, that of 1952 had added a star to the drill site in the mountain woods.

◁ LAOS

Paddy fields next to a forest accompany a motorway leading to a huge waterworks.

137

BOLIVIA

The sun shines on the mountain in Potosi where silver is found. In the foreground an alpaca, a breadfruit tree, and a sheaf of grain.

NICARAGUA ▷

Within the triangle of Freemasonry, a Jacobite cap of liberty sheds its rays over the mountains embraced by the seas.

◁ ECUADOR

A merchant ship on the seas, behind it Mount Chimborazo beneath the signs of the Zodiac for the months of the 1845 revolution.

EL SALVADOR ▷

These arms are almost the same as those of Nicaragua. The date of liberty is shown above the volcanoes.

◁ NEPAL

Framed in rhododendrons, a sacred cow and a pheasant beneath sun and moon, in the mountain scenery of Nepal.

138

◁ COSTA RICA

Again the shared history of Central America makes its appearance, but only three mountains are shown.

COLUMBIA ▷

The cap of liberty separates cornucopias and pomegranate (New Granada) from the isthmus of Panama.

◁ LIBERIA

The seascape/nautical piece refers to the founding of a free state by Negroes released from slavery and to their aspirations.

CUBA ▷

The key symbolizing the position of Cuba in the Gulf of Mexico has been taken from the arms of the capital.

◁ SEYCHELLES

The badge with the fruit-bearing sea coconut palm and giant turtle became the arms of these islands in 1976.

BUILDINGS
AND UTENSILS

Human artifacts are governed by the same principle as all other charges on an armorial shield. And this principle is that no subject is too prestigious or too insignificant to be used as an armorial charge.

Among the articles of everyday use, different items of civilian clothing form a substantial part, most notably the sleeve. And particular attention is paid to the type with a pocket attached, perhaps for a prayerbook. The English once again are masters in the graphic development of the outline of this sleeve. Because of its curious shape the French call it *manche mal taillée*, the English simply "maunche." Even in pieces of clothing one can find subjects for canting arms. A pair of open breeches is the sign of the Dutch family Abenbroek. Eating utensils

The famous Armorial Roll of Zurich is an example of the fact that the arms of distant countries were not always correctly represented. Thus the arms of Spain and Portugal shown here are useful only insofar as they show a "castle" for Castile and a "portal" for Portugal.

Below: An almost unlimited number of artifacts appear in heraldry, and the medieval heraldic artists, particularly the English, seemed to have a boundless imagination. Three musical instruments, "clarions" or "claricords"; three spoons, as canting arms for one John Sponeley; and three stockings.

are seldom found as charges. In England, however, a surgical instrument known as a "fleam"—an ancient form of lancet—is more frequently found. Being English it is naturally stylized, so that it appears somewhat like a figure seven.

With the spread of heraldry beyond the circle of knights, the number of arms with tools and implements on them increased. The range included everything from agriculture —plowshares and also whole plows—to the tools of small-scale handicrafts. These implements did not only appear in the arms of people who plied a particular trade, but also in the arms and banners of guilds. These were often combined with the arms of a particular place, so that there were very few general arms of a particular trade or profession. The smiths and the painters are two examples of occupations for which there were special arms.

Naturally, several objects of utility from different sources can be combined in one shield. An example is the table of the guild of tanners of Solothurn shown on this page, where we see both a plow (denoting origin) and a tanner's knife

(denoting the trade). Among the less clearly discernible figures is the tile-making form which appears in the arms of families with names like Ziegler (tile is *Ziegel* in German). The rope-maker's hooks, on which ropes are twisted, will be apparent only to the expert.

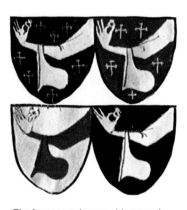

The four escutcheons with maunches—sleeves with a pocket for a prayer book—belonged to vassals of the elector of Trier and do not show that they were related but that they shared a common feudal status.

Right: Although encased in armor, the king of Castile and Leon is immediately recognizable because his arms are repeated on his surcoat, trappings, and crest. From a fifteenth-century manuscript.

The tools consisting of shafts have a certain resemblance to the private marks of medieval times. The fact that these private marks show a certain formal resemblance to runes led to wild speculation in the years after World War I that the origin of heraldry itself might be found in the runes. But the similarity between runes and merchant's marks exists only in the technique used, the lines being carved across the grain of the wood. Because of this, private marks have no curved lines, only angular corners.

Private marks do not appear in classical arms, and practically none have been granted containing one of these marks. In Polish and Lithuanian heraldry small objects such as horseshoes, arrows, and the like are typical. How far there is a connection with the Tatar house signs *(tamga)* which are still used in central Asia, for instance over the threshold of their tents, has yet to be seriously investigated. Such signs, like the types of merchant's mark, have their own specific meaning and they were often misunderstood in western Europe. An example of this misinterpretation appears in the arms of Lithuania.

The marklike sign of the dukes of Lithuania was often referred to as the gate with three towers. This led Konrad Grünenberg of Constance to give the knight an incorrectly decorated shield in his version of their arms, showing three towers rising above a gate- or doorway. A similar error can be seen in the arms of Spain and Portugal (illustrated on page 140), showing a castle for Castile and a portal for Portugal.

BUILDINGS AND UTENSILS
IN NATIONAL COATS OF ARMS

BRUNEI ▷

The winged canopy has since 1959 been combined with two hands; the motto beneath reads: "Brunei, House of Peace."

◁ TUVALU

The Big House (maneapa) where the council meets stands on an island, surrounded by eight banana leaves and eight seashells.

CAMBODIA ▷

A factory building instead of a star, as Cambodia follows the lead of Viet-Nam. Before that, a rice plantation did the job.

◁ ANTIGUA

In the rays of the sun and on a black ground, sugar cane mills on the hills of islands with white beaches.

BOTSWANA ▷

Sorghum and an ox head with the mine works on a Bantu shield supported by two leopards.

◁ TRANSKEI

In the heraldic shield, a corncob, a cog-wheel, and an ox head with a roofing spar.

BELIZE ▷

A sailing ship and some of the tools used to cut mahogany timber.

◁ BAHAMAS

In 1971 the royal crown gave way to the rising sun and the British ship to Columbus's Santa Maria.

SURINAM ▷

In 1959 a palm tree was added to the sailing ship with its centuries-old tradition and beside it, two American Indians.

◁ GABON

The national colors, and the ship of state of black Africa beneath the symbols of rich mineral resources.

146

◁TUNISIA

"Order, Freedom, and Justice," as the motto explains, the meaning of the Punic ship, the scales, and the lion.

KUWAIT▷

The popular falcon bearing the picture of a dhow and on its breast a shield in the same design as the national flag.

◁ST. KITTS-NEVIS-ANGUILLA

The bar separates two Poinciana flowers from a schooner; above is the head of a Caribbean between British badges.

QATAR▷

The dhow beside two palm trees competes for place as the insignia with the brown and white national flag.

◁MAURITIUS

"Star and Key to the Indian Ocean," the island was again granted its arms in 1906, heraldically revised.

147

ANDORRA ▷

Miter, crozier, and four pales for the Bishop of Urgel; three pales and the cows for France.

◁ TRINIDAD AND TOBAGO

In a shield in the national colors, two colibris are hovering over three ships from the fleet of Columbus.

SWEDEN ▷

King Albrecht of Mecklenburg first used the three crowns as his seal in 1364. The reason for this is not known.

◁ VATICAN CITY

The tiara, or triregnum, is placed above two crossed keys—one to bind and one to set free.

ETHIOPIA ▷

A swing plow, which men pull by a rope, before the sun and a cogwheel, with the old lion beneath.

◁ RHODESIA

The arms, granted in 1924, combine a hoe with items from Cecil Rhodes's posthumous arms.

SWAZILAND ▷

The Bantu shield of the Emasotsha regiment is placed between a lion and an elephant in the heraldic shield.

◁ CONGO (BRAZZAVILLE)

Hammer and hoe represent the classes, led by a star, united in creating the new Congo.

SOLOMON ISLANDS ▷

The native shield comes from the arms of 1956; the harpoons are new. The tortoises have been included since 1947.

◁ GAMBIA

The symbolism of Gambia is entirely agricultural, with axe and hoe crossed in blue.

149

ANGOLA ▷

Corn, coffee, cotton and part of a cog-wheel surround the sun behind a bush with machete and hoe.

◁ RWANDA

An agricultural community needs the pruning knife and hoe; the bow and arrow serve in defence of peace (dove).

MADAGASCAR (MALAGASY REPUBLIC) ▷

In the sun's rays above the sea, three arrowheads above rifle, shovel, and pen nib.

◁ OMAN

The two crossed swords in their sheath are crossed with the Gambia dagger and the sword belt(s).

MOZAMBIQUE ▷

Above the map by the ocean, hoe and automatic rifle are crossed over a book, with the radiant sun behind.

150

ISRAEL▷

The menorah, the seven-armed candelabra, is shown as on the Titus Arch, as Roman booty.

◁CAMEROON

Sword and scales have been replaced by a hand holding a torch before the map; above is the star of unity.

FRANCE▷

The democratic fasces of the lictors served as a symbol since the Revolution. The present design dates from 1929.

◁URUGUAY

The shield, quartered in the national colors, bears symbols of justice, strength, freedom, and prosperity.

SOVIET UNION▷

Hammer and sickle have appeared before the globe since 1924. The figures and texts of the motto change according to circumstances.

◁ TANZANIA

Lance, axe, and hoe were added to the torch on union with Tanganyika.

GERMAN DEMOCRATIC REPUBLIC (GDR) ▷

Agricultural, industrial, and intellectual workers are represented by the wreath of corn, the hammer, and the compasses.

◁ SIERRA LEONE

Above the ''lion mountains'' in heraldic style, three torches are lit for enlightenment in Africa.

BOTSWANA ▷

The cogwheels signify the desire for industrial development, but cattle farming still predominates.

◁ YUGOSLAVIA

The six torches represent the six constituent republics; from 1944 to 1963 there were only five, representing nationalities.

◁ BURMA
The cogwheel was added to the arms of 1948 (map) in 1974; the lion gave way to the large five-pointed star.

UGANDA▷

The sun shining upon the equator is placed above a drum, attribute of the former power of kings.

◁ PORTUGAL

Since 1910, King Manuel's celestial globe is shown around the traditional five "quinas" surrounded by castles.

NAURU▷

The symbol for phosphorus stands for guano; the souls of the ancestors dwell in the frigate bird which is shown beside the Tomano flowers.

◁ IRELAND

Henry VIII thought a harp was the old armorial sign for Ireland, and since then it has been so.

153

the helmet

Any device made of stiff material and intended to protect the head (and particularly the skull) against external injury may be described as a helmet. The helmets which were responsible for the invention of heraldry covered the face either completely or to such an extent that the person inside could not be adequately identified. The English archers and crossbowmen were much feared as opponents in later wars, having possibly learned their

Funeral helmet of the Emperor Charles V, 1558.
A battle scene around 1330 from a contemporary illustration. It shows the two basic forms of helmet. The

Right: Knight's spouse placing the helmet on his head before a tournament. The knight in the picture is wooing the lady, as is evident from the stylized letter A *(= Amor)* on his armorial coat.

iron hat with its broad brim left the face free. The closed helmet with its traplike visor could be opened during pauses in the battle for the wearer to take breath, as it would get very hot inside.

skill from the Saracens. By 1200, people had come to recognize the need for better face protection. In the process, however, they gave up one

154

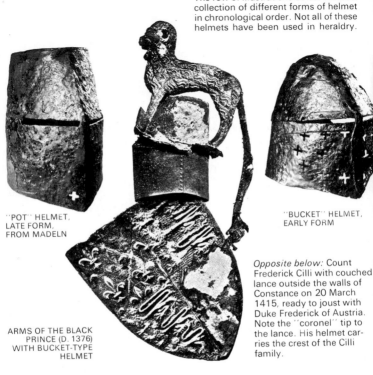

"POT" HELMET, LATE FORM, FROM MADELN

"BUCKET" HELMET, EARLY FORM

ARMS OF THE BLACK PRINCE (D. 1376) WITH BUCKET-TYPE HELMET

Opposite below: Count Frederick Cilli with couched lance outside the walls of Constance on 20 March 1415, ready to joust with Duke Frederick of Austria. Note the "coronel" tip to the lance. His helmet carries the crest of the Cilli family.

technical advantage, probably without being aware of it. For the helmets used up to this time were tapered off to a cone at the top, and in this way sword blows aimed at the wearer's head would often slide off. No doubt it was due to the iron-working techniques of the time that this shape was abandoned.

The new type of helmet was quite flat on top and looked like an inverted pot placed over the wearer's head. A slit was left for the eyes, the nose piece was reinforced and sometimes ornamentally decorated. The cheeks were covered by plates running right down to the chin instead of the simple ear flaps used previously. The wearer of such a helmet could only breathe with difficulty through the air holes left in the cheeks. Thus it was a great improvement when the front part could be opened like a cupboard door. For this it was first of all necessary to be able to make hinges. Contemporary poets sang at length of the broad reinforcing bands, which were often gilded. But

JOUSTING HELMET,
FLORENTINE MADE

HELMET FOR MACE
TOURNEYING

BARRED HELMET,
LATE FORM

nobody mentioned the fact that a sword blow on top of the potlike helmet could have fatal consequences for the wearer.

More than a century was to pass before a return to the conical shaping of the top plates of the helmet, providing much better protection against sword blows. The increased weight of this new type of helmet, which had something of the shape of an inverted bucket, was made easier to bear by extending the sides downward so that the helmet rested on the wearer's shoulders. Here the force of the enemy's sword could do less damage than it could on the top of the head.

Two separate lines of development appeared at that time. The first was purely military,

the second more sporting. Fighting as a sport was carried on in tournaments arranged in the traditional manner. It was more important for the development of heraldry than proper military wars.

In war, which increasingly made use of paid soldiers in-stead of feudal conscripts, the armor used was relatively simple. There was an iron hat which had a broad brim to protect the wearer against sword blows and left the face free, making for easier breath-ing and general mobility. Breathing seems to have been

Below: The detail from the Gothic folding table of Lüneburg (around 1330) shows the arms of the king of France *(left)* with the crest of Emperor Ludwig of Bavaria and the arms of the king of Bohemia.

a great problem in helmets. A further improvement on the "bucket" helmet was the movable visor which raised to open and was easier to use than the flap which opened like a cupboard door. This new visor fitted in with the general development of Gothic art, in which pointed forms tended to predominate.

Thus the jousting helmet was

The so-called Prank helmet (ca. 1350) is one of the few well-preserved examples of its kind. It comes from Seckau in Austria.
Technically, this helmet represents an important advance. The five steel plates from which it is made are brought together into a cone shape at the top, so that sword-blows are likely to slip off. Such an elaborate crest would only be worn in a tournament and not in a real battle.

Left: The armorial of Konrad Grünenberg shows the typical forms of mantling. Here we see *(left to right):* material in strips; material with scalloped edges; a similar pattern but with the metal side outward as the mantling is joined directly to the crest; strips of material with a decorative pattern of folds.

created. It extended into a point at the front and was used for jousting—the form of tourneying in which combatants with lances tried to knock each other from their horses. In order to meet the demands of this type of activity, the connection between the helmet and the rest of the armor was gradually made more secure. As an improvement on this unreliable type of join, the front part of the helmet was

159

Right: It is doubtful whether the minnesinger Wolfram von Eschenbach is shown here with his real arms. It seems unlikely that he would have exchanged what are usually assumed to be his family arms (flowers in a pot with handles) for the battle axes in order to please a lady. Perhaps it was the other way round, and it is the flowers in the pot which were adopted as a symbol of love. In any case the picture shows clearly how a pole-shaped crest could conveniently be attached to the side of the "pot" helmet. Shield, crest, and banner all carry the same design.

elongated so that what was now the jousting helmet could be firmly screwed together with the armor of the upper part of the body. The form of the helmet which resulted became the standard model of the heraldic helmet for the next few centuries.

Instead of the helmet being fastened to the body armor by means of its breastplate, it could be arranged that the lower part of the helmet was no longer attached to the helmet itself, but formed part of the body armor, which was extended upward. The helmet then only consisted of the upper part, in which case it was known by the French name of *salade*. Like other names given to helmet shapes, this derives from its similarity to an item of kitchen equipment. Apart from pot and bucket helmets, there was also the little basin or basinet, which was worn under the actual fighting helmet. One often sees on gravestones a representation of the buried man wearing a basinet, with his battle or tourneying helmet lying by his head.

The *salade* is difficult to use as an heraldic helmet because without shoulder pieces it cannot rest on an armorial shield. For this reason there are very few examples of a *salade* being

V. MÜLHEIM.

V. MÜLHEIM.

V. MÜL HEIM.

Some families with many ramifications used different crests to identify the different lines. Among the most inventive were two Alsatian families, the noble von Müllenheims with twenty-four variants in the so-called Siebmacher armorial.

used. In existing cases, a chin piece has had to be added.

The change from jousting with lances to tourneying with maces, when the object was merely to strike off the op-

The physical appearance of the knight on horseback *(below)* shows exactly the arrangement of the diagonally placed shield with the helmet on top which became customary in heraldic representations of arms. He is wearing a typically German crest.

emperor, other principles were developed based on attitudes which were even more favorable to the nobility or more democratic, as the case might be.

The art forms of the Renaissance were not favorable to the depiction of armorial helmets, but they did not disappear from heraldic art.

In the heyday of heraldry, crests on helmets played a highly decorative role. Because of the comblike shape of these early helmet decorations, they are all known in English as crests. The equivalent word in German, *Schirmbrett,* applies only to the

ponent's crest, brought further alterations. The field of vision was enlarged and only a few bars were used to protect the face. The use of this "barred" helmet was restricted by the imperial chancellery in Germany to the nobility as upholders of the tradition of tourneying. This privilege was also shared by certain people who enjoyed the same standing as the nobility, for example those who had a doctor's title in law or theology. In countries not subject to the jurisdiction of the German

fan crest, while all others are known by the name of *Helmzier*—"helmet decoration."

The increasing splendor of helmets and their decorations reflected the tone of the chival-

rous way of life, which reached its apogee in courtly tournaments. The people of the time looked upon crests as an artistic form of decoration. They called them gems, or *Zimier*, after the French *cimier*, a word derived from *cime*, summit.

In referring to the pictorial sources from the Middle Ages, however, one must always consider whether they represent real or ideal examples. This remains true up to a point even today—one finds illustrations of ceremonial gar-

162

A review of helmets, detail. A free-lance herald hired for the occasion inspects the helmets of the participants in a tournament; their escutcheons are painted on the necks of the helmets. Konrad Grünenberg's Armorial, 1483.

ments which could only be worn in theory.

The form of the crest affects the way it is graphically represented. The real helmet can of course be seen from all sides. In transferring it to paper, some reflection is required to determine how the most favorable overall effect can be achieved. One factor to be borne in mind is that the crest should appear on the same axis as the helmet. This was

true for the pot-shaped helmet and remained so for the bucket-shaped helmet. Both helmets are easily represented, from the side as well as from the front. So long as the crest consists of only a single figure, such as a branch, for example,

it does not matter which aspect of the helmet is shown on paper, for a branch can be represented equally well from all angles. This is true also of a set of bells mounted on a shaft, or similar contrivances which were later misinterpreted.

The mantling, initially only a piece of colored cloth covering the back of the neck and helmet, is thought to have originated in the hot climate of the Near East. The more heraldry shifted from actuality to a graphic plane, the more textile fashions influenced the helmet mantling, which apart from a few "aberrations" may always be assumed to be made of cloth. So the helmet mantling gained a graphic function which arose not from its origins but from the artistic currents of the various epochs. Apart from the formal ele-

The full achievement of arms of the kingdom of Aragon with a dragon issuant for a crest *(left)*. In accordance with the exaggeration of the late Gothic style, the mantling is slashed into deep fringes with tassels at the ends. Decoration of the mantling can also take the form of small designs on one or even both sides of the material. The motifs can be derived either from the crest (as with the lozenges, *center*), or from the shield (the billets and "water bougets," *right*).

ment, the helmet mantling is also to be considered as an element of color.

With the growth of national consciousness in Europe, the social structure changed radically, along with its exterior manifestations. This was particularly noticeable in the val-ue attached to the crest. In Italy, the country which can be regarded as the birthplace of the Renaissance, until around 1500 crests were particularly impressive in design and execution. The great families vied with one another in the invention of different crests for

The arms of Nils Ereng-nislesson of Hammer-sta from his painted bookplate, 1409—1440. The helmet, a transitional form between the ''bucket'' helmet and the jousting helmet, carries a mant-ling which is still seen as a straightforward strip of cloth with arbi-trary colors.

Right: Albrecht Dürer strove for realism even in his heraldic draw-ings. His helmet mant-ling is always treated so that it appears almost three-dimensional. In the arms of the noble von Rogendorfs, the crests of the Rogendorf arms (buffalo horns with peacock feathers) and the Wildhausen arms (lion issuant crowned) are combined on a single helmet.

different occasions. Thus the Viscontis either bore the same snake on their helmet as they did on their shield, or they bore the snake and a red tree as well.

Gothic forms not only made possible the bearing of helmets and crests without the addition of a shield, but also created an optical top-heaviness, especially when the three-cornered shield was replaced by the rectangular jousting shield. The architectonic forms of the Renaissance, on the other hand, did not lend themselves to the further development of this style.

the crown

Coins bearing portraits of rulers

Ptolemy V Epiphanos
(204—180 B.C.).

Julius Caesar (100—44 B.C.).

Napoleon I, Emperor of the French
(reigned 1804—1815).

Whatever social order man creates for himself, it always has at its summit a supreme representative, whether he is called chief, prime minister, commander-in-chief, king, or king of kings, or emperor.

A narrow cloth band worn round the forehead and at the back of the neck was considered an adequate sign of status by the kings of the ancient Near East. The Greek word *diadem,* which is used today for a sumptuous head ornament, in fact only means "bound together," from διαδέω ("I bind together"). The loose ends of the royal diadems from Asia Minor (see Ptolemy V, top left) still emphasized the spiritual nature of kingship everywhere, at a time when the narrow cloth band had become a gold circle set with precious stones. In the "heraldic" ear, this change-over was already an historical fact.

The cultural collapse of Europe which accompanied the popular migrations of the

Portrait of the legendary King Arthur.
On his clothing and the pennant of
his lance he bears the arms attributed
to him by posterity, consisting of
three crowns.

post-Roman era was followed
in the eighth century by a
turning back to the values of
antiquity. This process was
achieved with difficulty, since
it had to be built on facts
which had been almost completely forgotten.

In the heyday of heraldry,
from the thirteenth to the fifteenth century, there was a
standard crown consisting of a
headband on which four
leaves were mounted, one over
the forehead, one at the back,
and one over each cheek. In
heraldic depictions one leaf is
completely visible, and two
leaves each half-visible. Kings
were represented wearing this
type of crown even under cir-

crowns of the kings of Asia Minor imitate the rays of the sun. In ancient Egypt, before sun worship was replaced by idolatry, the sun's disk invariably appeared in the tall feathered constructions which served as crowns.

The closeness between priesthood and kingship is shown by the headgear worn by the kings of Asia Minor. But the military commander-in-chief and emperor could also be the same person. The emperors of ancient Rome were literally

cumstances where they would not actually be able to wear it, for instance while lying down asleep. A crown of this kind became a symbol of royal dignity to such an extent that many princes, when taking over newly won lands as their kingdoms, simply used one or more crowns as their arms, when there were none already in existence.

All the pre-Christian rulers justified their wielding of power by ascribing it to higher forces. The unification of the two parts of ancient Egypt was expressed by the joining of the two crowns which the two protecting goddesses had previously worn separately. The

called "commander"—*imperator*. They wore a plain laurel wreath of pure gold and this may be derived from the veneration of victors in sport-

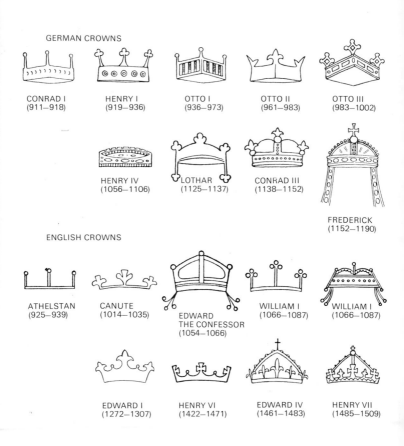

Up to the fourteenth century, the royal crowns were too varied in form to show any real development. A look at these German and English crowns taken from seals and book illustrations makes this clear.

GERMAN CROWNS

CONRAD I
(911—918)

HENRY I
(919—936)

OTTO I
(936—973)

OTTO II
(961—983)

OTTO III
(983—1002)

HENRY IV
(1056—1106)

LOTHAR
(1125—1137)

CONRAD III
(1138—1152)

FREDERICK
(1152—1190)

ENGLISH CROWNS

ATHELSTAN
(925—939)

CANUTE
(1014—1035)

EDWARD
THE CONFESSOR
(1054—1066)

WILLIAM I
(1066—1087)

WILLIAM I
(1066—1087)

EDWARD I
(1272—1307)

HENRY VI
(1422—1471)

EDWARD IV
(1461—1483)

HENRY VII
(1485—1509)

ing events who wore a real laurel wreath as a sign of victory.

The name of Julius Caesar and the title of *imperator* have come to signify a status above that of king. When the title emperor was revived by the French in the nineteenth century, its holders adorned their heads with the ancient laurel wreath not only on coins but also at ceremonial appearances. Napoleon I was perfect-

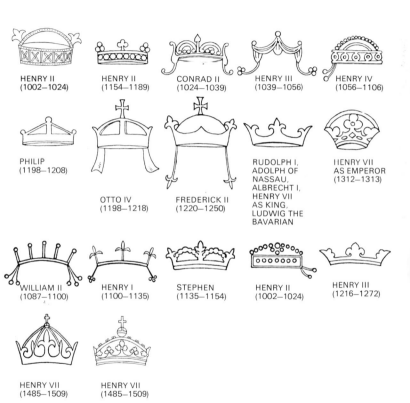

HENRY II
(1002–1024)

HENRY II
(1154–1189)

CONRAD II
(1024–1039)

HENRY III
(1039–1056)

HENRY IV
(1056–1106)

PHILIP
(1198–1208)

OTTO IV
(1198–1218)

FREDERICK II
(1220–1250)

RUDOLPH I,
ADOLPH OF
NASSAU,
ALBRECHT I,
HENRY VII
AS KING,
LUDWIG THE
BAVARIAN

HENRY VII
AS EMPEROR
(1312–1313)

WILLIAM II
(1087–1100)

HENRY I
(1100–1135)

STEPHEN
(1135–1154)

HENRY II
(1002–1024)

HENRY III
(1216–1272)

HENRY VII
(1485–1509)

HENRY VII
(1485–1509)

ly logical in establishing this connection with ancient Rome, for his empire had developed from a republic like that of the Caesars in Rome. Until the thirteenth century, there was no system to the design of royal and imperial crowns. The jewels which occasionally appear hanging from short chains over the wearer's ears reveal an oriental influence. In the Western world, rank and degree also came to be expressed in the shape and adornment of the crown. A hoop over the basic crown became the sign of an emperor, and the holiness of the empire soon came to be expressed by the addition of a bishop's miter, turned through ninety degrees so that the imperial hoop passed between the horns of the miter. For a long time this form of crown was evidently restricted to the Holy Roman Empire of the Germanic nations—there may perhaps have been a parallel form inspired by Charlemagne in France. This type of crown became the pattern for imperial crowns, when other emperors appeared besides the German Roman emperor, in particular the czars in Moscow.

In 1525 Charles I of Spain ordered that the crown closed with arches as a symbol of sovereignty should be reserved for the king, and the leaf crown should be assigned to the Spanish grandees.

The hoops arching above the head of the crowned sovereign were regarded as the symbol of sovereignty and became increasingly important in the hierarchy of crowns which developed during the Renaissance. This can be observed in the development of electoral hats. The German electors had an official costume which they actually wore, part of which was a purple cap rimmed with ermine.

After the treaties of Westphalia (1648), electors' hats, or coronets, were also closed with hoops, a development followed by the prince's coronet (see page 178), which is wholly equal in status to a prince's crown. The hoops arching above the head were invariably decorated with a closely

The head reliquary of Charlemagne *(left)* in the cathedral treasure at Aix-la-Chapelle bears an imperial sign in the hoop passing from front to back of the head. This matches the so-called imperial crown *(bottom)*, first commissioned by Otto I the Great for his coronation as emperor in 962.

set row of pearls and normally surmounted by a mound or orb.

From the Renaissance onward, pearls joined the leaf shapes on the circlet as principal indicators of rank. They were first mounted directly on the circlet, numerous pearls being used for a high-ranking noble such as a count, and a small number for a lower-ranking one such as a baron. Chains of pearls wrapped around the circlet were also fashionable. From the eighteenth century, certain rules came to be established.

Crowns are occasionally found as grave ornaments in the tombs of kings and are often remarkably unpretentious, as, for example, in the imperial tombs of Speyer. Sometimes these graves include remarkable trinkets which a royal person has worn or greatly valued during his or her life. Examples are the so-called crown cap of the empress Constance, and even more remarkable, the Castilian royal crown found in Toledo.

The German imperial crown, which up to the nineteenth century was generally believed to have been worn by Charlemagne himself, was transported from one repository to another in the Middle Ages; whoever possessed it was the legitimate ruler. In 1424 the emperor Sigismund created a permanent storage place for it in Nuremberg, whence it had to be brought by special envoys for each coronation, which took place first in Aix-la-Chapelle and then in Frankfurt.

Once the need had arisen in representative art for realistic portraiture of people, this also

had an effect on crowns. They were no longer fashioned without reference to the people who were to wear them. Neither the Stephen nor the Wenceslas crown were "ordered" by the kings after whom they are named, but they were given a more individual style.

The crown cap of the empress Constance, the wife of the emperor Friederick II. This type of crown, known as a "kamelaukion," is completely eastern Roman, as can be seen from the latticed side pendants.

The German imperial crown offers an impressive early example of this. The imperial crown with a hoop between the horns of a miter could be regarded as a norm as early as the fourteenth and fifteenth centuries. It was left to an artistically minded emperor to have a work of art made from this model according to his personal requirements. In 1602 the emperor Rudolph II had an imperial crown made in his world-famous court workshops at Prague, which represented four scenes from his life on the external sides of the miter.

Many crowns were quite simply melted down for their metal. This was especially the case with overthrown monarchies. There were many losses of this kind in France, where only a few crowns escaped destruction. A coronation is a unique event in the life of a monarch. Multiple coronations were an exception which nevertheless took place; for instance in the case of Richard I, Cœur de Lion, who had himself crowned a second time after defeating his treacherous brother, and in that of those German Roman emperors who were also kings of Hungary and Bohemia.

STEPHEN'S
CROWN
OF HUNGARY

IMPERIAL CROWN
OF AUSTRIA

HERALDIC CROWN
OF THE KINGDOM OF ITALY

ST. EDWARD'S
CROWN OF ENGLAND

IMPERIAL CROWN
OF RUSSIA

CROWN OF THE
KINGDOM OF PRUSSIA

PERIAL STATE CROWN
OF GREAT BRITAIN

CROWN OF THE CROWN
PRINCE OF SWEDEN

STEEL CROWN
OF THE KINGDOM
OF RUMANIA

177

CROWNS AND CORONETS OF RANK

	KING	PRINCE (CROWN)	PRINCE (CORONET)
FRANCE Only members of the royal house can wear fleurs-de-lis on the head-band of their crowns.			
SWEDEN The Swedish system is basically the most conservative.			
SPAIN The Spanish system is built up consistently.			
ITALY The Italian rules take into consideration the fact that many families hold titles from the German Roman Empire.			
GERMANY Ordinarily there is no difference between the crowns of a duke and a prince. Counts with the title of "illustrious" are a creation of the post-Napoleonic restoration.			
NETHERLANDS The Dutch hierarchy of crowns shows influences from all the neighboring states.			
BELGIUM SINCE 1838 After the creation of the kingdom of Belgium many Dutch rules remained in force.			
ENGLAND The English hierarchy is strictly observed. Princely coronets exist but vary with relationship to the sovereign. The coronet caps are optional.			

DUKE	"ILLUSTRIOUS" COUNT	MARQUIS	COUNT, NORMAL	COUNT OR EARL, PERMITTED

179

VISCOUNT	BARON, NORMAL	BARON, PERMITTED	KNIGHT	UNTITLED NOBL NORMAL

*" . . . So that you may be considered
among the ranks of well-known fighters and decorated
with the precious stones of virtue,
and crowned with the reward
of eternal happiness . . . "*
(from an inauguration speech, ninth century)

Above: Crown of an English princess, probably Blanche of
Lancaster, the daughter of King Henry IV (d. 1437). *Below:*
The crown of King Christian IV of Denmark, 1596.

heraldic accessories

Supporters in the true sense of the word, these two ladies, recognizable by their richly folded garments, are found as early as 1292 on the seal of Heinrich von Scharfeneck. They flank the shield and hold it with outstretched arms, each gracefully decorating its upper edge with a noble flower.

Few sovereigns can resist the impression of splendor afforded by a pair of heraldic beasts supporting their coat of arms. These beasts can be borrowed from the coat of arms itself, as in the case of the kingdom of Bavaria *(right)*, or they can be one of the pictorial badges which are displayed by the ruler in other contexts.

SUPPORTERS

Every portrait of an armigerous lord with his shield shows a kind of shield bearer who may be looked on as a forerunner of the "supporter." The latter has in the course of time developed into an integral part of the coat of arms. Of the some 160 sovereign states of the world, almost a third bear arms with supporters in the strictest sense (i.e., one on either side of the shield). It is increasingly becoming the custom for the supporters to consist of animals of two different species. No animal can compete with the lion, however, which is generally preferred as a supporter.

It may be assumed that the souvenir print published in Bruges in 1468 (see page 101) contributed much to the heraldic lion's becoming such a favorite supporter.

The development of supporters is best traced through seals. The representation on the seal

of its possessor is older than heraldry. As soon as a shield or the complete armorial bearings could be considered to identify a person, the shield or the armorial bearings would also appear in the appropriate place on the seal. In view of its legal validity, a seal was bound to encompass all the elements which would support its authenticity.

In view of the concept that the arms or the armorial beast directly represented the armiger, near-heraldic beings appear on seals, particularly those which are identical to or related to a badge. The space between the shield and the edge of the seal is ideally suited to the insertion of small animal reliefs, which spring not so much from the whim of the engraver as from the intentions of the person who commissioned the seal. These figures were obviously not chosen purely on the grounds of *horror vacui* or the need for symmetry.

The *horror vacui* (abhorrence of empty space) plays a not inconsiderable role in seal engraving, since a plain, unengraved surface does not imprint well in sealing wax or wax. An empty background can be damasked just like the field on a coat of arms and fill-

ed out with a lattice or scroll pattern. If figures of men or beasts are chosen instead of this, a particular significance can be attached to them, though such seals are admittedly rare. Almost every seal on which the space between the shield and the edge is filled with figures must therefore be looked at individually in order to establish what motive may have led to the choice of these accompanying figures.

It is not always just a question of filling the space between the edge of the armorial shield and the inscription running round the circular seal. There are also trefoils and quatrefoils

Below: The supporters of the arms of England gradually ceased to change under Henry VII. During the last three Tudor reigns, the English lion stood on the right and the Welsh dragon of the Tudors on the left.

Overleaf: In historic galleries of ancestors, the figures act as supporters for their own arms. On the fourteenth-century windows of St. Stephen's cathedral in Vienna, the eagle of Rudolph (d. 1291) is turned politely toward that of his bearded son Albrecht I (d. 1308).

The colonizer of Maryland, Lord Baltimore, bequeathed his arms to the naissant state. The feudal-style leopard supporters, however, were replaced by local inhabitants, a plowman and a fisherman. The "male chauvinist" Italian motto—"Deeds are a man's, words a woman's affair"—was allowed to remain.

The almost naturalistic "Marzocco" lion with the arms of Florence under its right forepaw is a masterpiece by

Donatello, originally intended for the papal apartments in the monastery of Maria Novella (ca. 1416).

and similar multiform shapes, the angles and arches of which are occupied by small figures. On the seal of Catherine of Savoy-Vaud, Countess of Namur (1352), there are the symbols of the four evangelists. On that of Isabel of Chalon-Arlay, mistress of Vaud (1338), we find music-playing melusines, a reference to the blood-relationship with the Cypriot royal house of

Above: Two copper plates by Martin Schongauer (1450—1491): A servant with the escutcheons of his masters; angel supporting religious arms. Lion showing his extremities round the edge of the shield; Wyvern representing the Welsh dragon. From *Tesserae Gentilitiae* by Silvestre Petra Sancta, Rome, 1638.

Lusignan, together with eagles and lions from Savoyard heraldry.

Without venturing to establish a chronological order, we will now take a look at some groups of supporters established by the study of seals.

The simplest method of depositing a shield somewhere in from a tree fork or branch, and this arrangement was emphasized by the clear representation of the shield strap.

In Germany shields sitting in the tops of trees are a typical feature of old municipal arms. In many of them the shield is clearly hung from a branch by its strap. The living figures ap-

a more or less decorative fashion is to hang it from a hook on the wall or on a tree—there is technically no difference between the two. Ladies who used not to bear a helmet and crest frequently showed their unaccompanied shield hung pearing on many badges also proved ideal supporters, provided they did not appear with their backs turned to the shield and did more than merely touch it. Their decorative effect was recognized no later than around 1290.

A shield is held while standing or sitting, in the latter case on a throne or on a horse. The attitude taken up while doing this influenced the way of combining the shield and helmet so decisively that the slanting position of the shield has remained the normal one to this day. The sight of an armed soldier was so familiar in the Middle Ages that the reclining figure of a dead man was depicted as though he were standing. At his feet was a lion or a hound while his head was framed by a pediment or even a fully sculpted baldachin.

Once the restricting frame of the seal was removed from the representation of the human figure, the supporter could be placed on a ground and from ornamental considerations this developed into an architecturally constructed pedestal, called a compartment. In blazons such compartments are usually mentioned but not described. In periods of overflowing artistic forms such as the Renaissance, baroque, and rococo, use was made of the possibilities provided by this freedom. The placing of supporters on a compartment can add to the impression of pomp

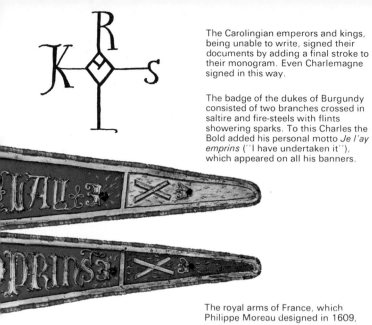

The Carolingian emperors and kings, being unable to write, signed their documents by adding a final stroke to their monogram. Even Charlemagne signed in this way.

The badge of the dukes of Burgundy consisted of two branches crossed in saltire and fire-steels with flints showering sparks. To this Charles the Bold added his personal motto *Je l'ay emprins* ("I have undertaken it"), which appeared on all his banners.

The royal arms of France, which Philippe Moreau designed in 1609,

given by a badge or coat of arms. The Prussian kings in the eighteenth century inscribed their motto *Gott mit uns* ("God with us") on a plinth richly decorated with royal eagles. Their princes on the other hand had to be content with a simple shelf, with the two wild men supporting the coat of arms maintaining the equilibrium. The wild men on the Danish coat of arms, by contrast, seem to be standing on cliffs.

Some mottoes become an integral part of the coat of arms, such as the *Dieu et mon droit*

incorporated all the armorial insignia for the first time. The kings' battle cry was indeed *Montjoie St. Denis,* and it is correctly placed above everything else.

191

The *Kurmainzer Landrecht (Provincial Law of the Electorate of Mainz)* was published in the year 1755 and decorated with the arms of the Archbishop with their four quarterings, two of them derived from the whippets of his family arms.

("God and my right") of the English King Henry V (reigned 1413–1422) and his successors. This was incorporated into the coat of arms with Henry VIII (reigned 1509–1547). When this is the case, the motto appears beneath the coat of arms on a fluttering banderole, which serves as a basis for the supporters. Alternatively it is inscribed on a plinth. Many of these mottoes were retained by the person's successors. Most of them, however, remained attached to the person who had chosen them, such as the motto *Je l'ay*

The tomb of an English knight with a recumbent lion serving as a footrest.

emprins (in modern French, *Je l'ai entrepris*—"I have undertaken it") which Charles the Bold (d. 1477) had inscribed on all his banners.

Admittedly the use of letters is forbidden in heraldry, as the sign should speak for itself without elucidation, but the ornamental possibilities of the shape of letters are not altogether lost. The kings of the Middle Ages devised their monograms out of skillfully combined letters, and such artistically designed words as the *Libertas* of the Italian city states are another illustration of this.

In the past few centuries, despite their personal character, mottoes have found their way into the heraldry of families. This has happened because, at least since the eighteenth century, the offices of particular orders, when asking a newly created knight for a proposal of arms to be inserted in the order's register, have also asked for details of his motto. In modern state arms, especially those which are influenced by British heraldry, compartments have also gained information value.

MANTLES
AND PAVILIONS

The state arms of a modern monarchy of European stamp appear in their most luxurious manifestation equipped with an armorial cloak or tent. This was possible in the form in which we understand it only

High-ranking lords did not renounce their customary comforts even on the battlefield. The illustration shows a negotiation scene in tents, fourteenth century. Bibliothèque Nationale, Paris.

since the seventeenth century. In 1609, a Bordeaux lawyer by the name of Philippe Moreau was compiling his *Tableau des* *armoiries de France*. He used the throne seals of kings as a model for sumptuously presented coats of arms. For this he re-

placed the figure of the king by his shield, which now appeared under a canopy of billowing material. The symbol of sovereignty above the shield found much approval among admirers of French customs, and a distinction was established between the armorial tent (with a dome) and the armorial cloak (without the dome). The armorial tent became a privilege of the ruler of the state, while the cloak was attributed to princes and princesses.

The prototype of the tent and cloak is not the robe worn by the monarch to his coronation, but the portable canopy of oriental potentates and of the pope as well as the fixed canopy over the throne of worldly and spiritual rulers. The princes of the Middle Ages frequently lived in tents suited to their rank, while engaged in sport or military campaigns.

The proper armorial cloak also developed out of the armorial surcoats which princes wore themselves and also had their heralds wear. These cloaks bear the complete image of the armorial shield, but only reveal those parts which are at the edge of the cloak, and even these are seen in re-

verse. The armorial cloaks and tents of princes are generally purple on the outside. They can be decorated with small motifs which may be derived from badges. These have existed since the fourteenth century and carry almost as much significance as the coat of arms itself. They evade systematization, but are among those elements of graphic art which can be very useful in establishing an object's date and provenance.

This applies not only to English badges but also to French *devises* and Italian *imprese*, particularly where these relate to particular princes and the period of their reign.

BADGES

The eighteen different badges of the "illustrious family of Stafford" were certified by Garter King of Arms in 1720. Half are on a half-black, half-red round; i.e., in the livery colors of the family.

Graphically, badges often cannot be distinguished from armorial charges; indeed the two are often identical. Badges have the advantage that they can be used in unlimited numbers, somewhat like a fabric pattern, as is the case with the French fleur-de-lis. For his coronation in 1483, Richard III of England is said to have ordered 13,000 white boars. These were to be distributed at the ceremony over the clothes of the doorkeepers and the king's retinue, who were dressed in "livery colors" decorated with badges.

Some very well known badges have even given their names to political factions, the best-known being the white rose of York, which represented the side of King Richard III in the Wars of the Roses. The conclusion of this war still finds expression today in the Tudor rose (see on page 198). In England the badges of prominent, politically influential personalities were at times so popular that Shakespeare could presuppose a knowledge of them in his historical plays. Originally the livery colors in which a lord dressed his servants were a matter of free choice, but they then tended to be maintained within a family. The dynasty of Lancaster used blue and white, the house of York blue and murrey (a mulberry color), the Tudors white and green, and the Stuarts gold and scarlet. In accordance with the now established heraldic rules, the ruling English dynasty uses red and yellow.

England and Italy are the countries in which the custom of using emblems other than the coat of arms itself has flourished most vigorously. Indeed it is still alive in England and its sphere of cultural influence.

Bronze door of the funeral chapel of King Henry VII in Westminster Abbey (1509) with the armorial charges of the royal house (fleurs-de-lis and lions) and its badges: a sunburst, a portcullis, a falcon and fetterlock, a crown, and the intertwined letters R and h.

Italian badges or *imprese* are of two kinds. In the first the picture is accompanied as above by a not always very informative motto on a fluttering band. In the second, the picture remains unexplained, and must have caused almost as much head-scratching among contemporary observers as among those of the present day, who seldom find an explanation. The scientific approach to *imprese* and other badges is still in its infancy, but at least there are some historically arranged collections now in existence. In order to

The strictness of heraldic rules led again and again to currents or whole eras in which additional badges appeared, won popularity, and then disappeared again. Many nations

JAPAN
Flags of coastal lords *(daimyo),* each bearing a *mon* in particular colors.
Nineteenth century.

ASANO,
DAIMYO AT HIROSHIMA

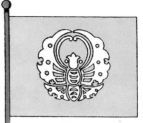

IKEDA,
DAIMYO AT OKAYAMA

ENGLAND
In England and its overseas possessions, the use of badges has persisted to the present day. Many of them have lasted over several generations.

TUDOR ROSE

JANE SEYMOUR,
3RD WIFE OF HENRY VIII

EDWARD

FRANCE
Relating to a single person only, the pictorial badges *(corps de devise)* in French heraldry are usually accompanied by a descriptive motto (the *âme de devise),* which often reflects attributions of the badge.

PORCUPINE
LOUIS XII

ERMINE, ANNE OF BRITTANY,
QUEEN OF FRANCE

SPAIN
Unframed images, partly taken from the coat of arms, have been used as near-heraldic badges in Spain from the twelfth century right up to the present.

YOKE (YUGO) OF
FERDINAND I

ARROWS (FLECHAS)
OF QUEEN ISABELLA

ST. JOHN'S EAG
OF ARAGON

have proved highly inventive in
this field, in particular Japan.

IKEDA, DAIMYO
AT OKAYAMA, VARIANT

UESUGI,
DAIMYO AT YONEZAWA

EIR APPARENT
TO THRONE

CATHERINE PARR,
6TH WIFE OF HENRY VIII

RICHMOND
HERALD

PORTCULLIS

HREE CROWNS
HENRY III

LOUIS XIV, THE SUN KING,
FORTRESS GATE AT LANDAU

EGRANATE AND
NGLISH ROSE

CATHERINE OF ARAGON
MARRIED HENRY VIII
IN 1509

FLINT AND STEEL

TWO BRANCHES
IN SALTIRE, ADOPTED
FROM THE FORMER
DUKEDOM
OF BURGUNDY

interpret the images, one requires an intimate knowledge of the world of fables and fairy tales and the proverbs of many ages.

Many pictures will appear quite obvious to a modern observer. A few examples will make this clear.

In a Milanese *imprese* an arm holding a bag obviously crammed with money emerges from clouds and rays of light indicating the "weather." The message is that the right time for giving money is *Qu(a)ndo sarà tempo*—when the time is right, or when the weather is right.

A mountain torrent is walled in at the sides. Motto: *Per più sigurez(z)a* ("for greater safety").

A man sits wailing on a small hill; a snake crawls out of his clothing and bites him on the right cheek. Motto: *Io levato la bis(ci)a in sene* ("I nourished the viper in my bosom").

A beehive aswarm with bees. Motto: *Per mel merito* ("for well-deserved honey").

A lamb lying on its back is bit-

in uso da Barnabo Vesscor —

ten in the neck by a wolf standing over it. Motto: *Che per gra se fa* ("what happens through mercy").

A bush with knotted branches. Motto: *Per non fallire* ("so as not to grow awry").

A fruit tree with grafting places. Motto: *Seg(u)ndo el tempo* ("at the appropriate time").

A horse lashing out backwards. Motto: *Vendet(t)a de tre(n)ta an(n)i* ("vengeance for thirty years").

A jousting shield leans against a boulder, with several smashed lances tipped with coronels lying in front of it. Motto: *Tu perde el tempo* ("you are wasting your time").

ORDERS AND DECORATIONS

When the term "order" is mentioned today, people immediately think of the crosses and medallions which are pinned to the chests of the survivors of wars as a mark of public gratitude for their services.

Order initially meant rule, statute, regulation—a regu-

1095 had to find some form of organization to make their lofty task possible. It went without saying that the Crusaders, in the hostile surroundings in which they found themselves, drew closer together and fought if possible beside those to whom they could express themselves.

lation to which a man freely submits and may carry some sign of on his clothing as a token of that submission. Those who "took the cross" in the wave of enthusiasm which gripped the Western world after the Council of Clermont in

Communal meal of the French Order of the Star. John II of France founded this order on 6 November 1351 in answer to the founding of the English Order of the Garter. The order was to consist of 500 knights, forming the backbone of the national army. Charles V let the order die out again.

AN ORDER OF CRUSADING
KNIGHTS
A member of the Order of the
Knights of St. John wearing the tunic
of the order.

A COURT ORDER
Duke Charles the Bold of Burgundy
as grand master of his Order of the
Golden Fleece, an order of knights
based on feudal loyalty.

These groupings were oriented toward the church by reason of their motivation, and could present a threat to the emergent kingdoms because of the military power incorporated in them. There were three possible solutions to this problem. First, the king could make himself the head of one of these orders, as happened in Spain and Portugal. Second, the king could attempt more or less totally to eliminate an order which had become too powerful, as did Philip the Fair of France in the years 1307–1314. Third, the king could himself set up an order into which he could draft reliable supporters. This was the origin of the courtly orders based on feudal loyalty, some of which have survived to this day, above all the English Order of the Garter.

This development was part of a progression toward a system of rewards relatively free of obligation, instead of the loyalty demanded by the original system. Under this system decorations were bestowed as a reward for merit; they were also called orders and accompanied by certain requirements, but even in the beginning they established only superficial relationships between the holders, and finally none at all. These are what are generally understood by the term order today, and their number has grown steadily since the eighteenth century. There is scarcely a country

SVERIGES SÄLLHET

CARL JOHAN
SVEA RIK: KRONPRINS

UTNÄMD
D: 2 | AUG: 1810

which has not taken part in this development since the French Republic abolished all royal orders and established that of the *Légion d'honneur*, thereby removing many objections to the existence of orders in a non-monarchic state.

A man who had taken the cross and, if his social standing permitted it, entered an order of knights, not only wore the cross on his clothing but also used it for his personal emblem, on his seal and on his shield.

The number of orders of knights which arose in the Holy Land and on the Iberian peninsula is considerable.

Three of them in particular
gained outstanding significance:

1. The Order of the Knights of
St. John traced its origin to a
hospital for the care of pilgrims which had already existed in Jerusalem some thirty
years before the first Crusade.
It was here that the crusading
knights founded a brotherhood after the taking of Jerusalem in 1099. The duties of
the order, originally restricted
to the care of sick soldiers, ex-
panded under Muslim pres-
sure to those of an order of
knights. This became very
clear long after the loss of the
Holy Land in 1291. In 1530
the order was invested with
the island of Malta as a base,
and from there it battled
against the North African pi-
rates, becoming known as the
"police of the Mediter-
ranean." Like all the other chivalrous orders which started in
Jerusalem, the Order of Malta, as it was generally known
after 1530, recognizes the pope
as its highest authority.

2. The Teutonic Order only
accepted "Germanic" mem-
bers, though this term covered
nationals of any of the countries belonging to the German
Roman empire. Its year of
foundation is generally regarded as 1190, for that is
when the crusading knights
besieged the fortress of Akko
(Acre). The knights of different orders were distinguished by the color of their cloaks
and the crosses sewn onto
them. The cloaks of the
knights of St. John were black
with white crosses, those of the

A carpet background showing Nicholas von Diesbach, lord of Signau, and his various orders, including the Order of the Sword of Cyprus, the Collar of SS of England, the Order of St. Catherine of Sinai (the toothed wheel), the Tankard Order of Aragon, the Order of the Swan of Cleves and the Order of the Holy Ghost or the Dove of Castile. His family arms appear on the shield and the horse blanket.

Teutonic knights the reverse. As a result the black cross potent which they wore has been considered the "Teutonic cross" right up to the present. From 1234 to 1525 a state created by this order existed on the Baltic; Prussia's claim

The inner sides of both doors of the church of St. Elizabeth in Marburg are painted with the arms of the grand master of the Teutonic Order of knights.

to sovereignty can be traced back to this time.

3. The mainly French-oriented Order of the Knights Templar was named after the temple of Solomon near its seat in Jerusalem, a picture of which appears on several seals of the order (see page 208). The order was founded approximately twenty years after the taking of Jerusalem and was distinguished by a white cloak with a red cross. The Templars were originally more intent on fighting the heathen than on the care of the sick, and confusion with the white cloaks of the Teutonic knights led to complaints being made to the Holy See, which was for both orders the highest authority. But the Pope could not protect them against Philip the Fair of France.

The bailiwick of Brandenburg of the Order of St. John separated from the main order on becoming Protestant. This factor, together with its close connection with the Hohenzollern dynasty, ruling at first in Brandenburg and then in Prussia, produced divergences in the design of the badge of the order and its linking with the family arms of the knights. A history of the Protestant Order of St. John brought out in 1728 gave an authoritative ruling in the matter.

1 Badge of the order
2 Scheme for commanders
3 Scheme for arms of one quarter
4 Scheme for quartered arms
5 Scheme for arms parted per fess
6 Scheme for quartered arms with inescutcheon
7 Scheme for arms parted per fess and in chief per pale with an inescutcheon

Right: On the Iberian peninsula the religious orders of knights contributed significantly to the expulsion of the Muslims. In Portugal the king was grand master of the Avis Order, whose green cross fleuretty he incorporated in his arms in such a way that only the fleurs-de-lis at the tips appear round the edge of the shield.

Below: The Order of the Knights Templar, destroyed between 1307 and 1314, was eventually very rich. In the beginning, however, it was apparently so poor that there was only one horse between every two knights,

The loss of the Holy Land to the Muslims did not affect the urge to ensure one's salvation by means of a pilgrimage, be it to Santiago de Compostela in Spain or to Palestine. The holy places remained accessible to pilgrims, who could be dubbed knights of the Holy Sepulcher at the tomb of Christ and then bear the cross of Jerusalem on their garments. On these pilgrimages, high-ranking lords would visit

as is shown on many of the order's seals.

Left: Heraldry of the Teutonic Order *(from left to right):* seal of the land master, 1244—1255; escutcheon of a landgrave of Hesse as a knight of the order; arms of the grand master; seal of the last grand master in Prussia, Albrecht of Brandenburg (until 1525).

The Sovereign Order of St. John of Jerusalem at Malta, named after its patron saint, John the Baptist, is a

religious order of knights generally known as the Order of Malta, after being given the island of Malta as a fief by the kingdom of Naples in 1530. Shown here are *(left to right):* seal of a commander from the year 1355; bookplate of a member of the Order of St. John (Knights of Malta) 1976, designed by Bruno Bernard Heim and engraved by Rudolf Niedballa; and seal of the English Order of St. John, established as a royal British Hospitaller Order in 1888. The actual arms were granted on 1 February 1926.

The archdukes of Austria from the line of Tuscany continued the traditions of the Grand Duchy of Tuscany when it was abolished in 1866, and with them the grandmastership of the Order of St. Stephen (red cross).

209

TEUTONIC ORDER OF
KNIGHTS

AVIS ORDER (Portugal)

the royal courts they passed on the way, in Cyprus for example, and receive other ceremonial orders. The status attached to these orders depended on the status of the person who conferred them.

The example of the kings of Cyprus was followed by many smaller potentates whose foundations could hardly compete in status with the Order of the Garter of the kings of England (probably founded in 1348), the Order of the Golden Annunciata of the dukes of Savoy (founded around 1360). Thus the margrave of Brandenburg created an Order of the Swan, which he dedicated to the Virgin Mary. A duke of Bourbon, although he was not a sovereign, created the Order of the Camail, the dukes of Austria an Eagle and a Dragon Order, and Emperor Sigismund the Dragon Order of Hungary, which was so popular there that its badge became transferable by inheritance. Many of these orders were destroyed by political developments or by the Reformation; also it became too difficult for the knights to make the expensive journeys to the chapter meetings. The statutes of a genuine order relate mainly to its internal life, and this could not be maintained without constant contact between the members. Even the highly regarded Order of the Golden Fleece held its last chapter—which means a meeting to discuss the affairs of the

ORDER OF THE GARTER
(England)

ORDER OF THE ELEPHANT
(Denmark)

order—in Bruges in the year 1555.

With the Renaissance, the development of orders took on a new and unfamiliar direction. They became increasingly a tool for political propaganda. The number of knights of the French Order of St. Michael (founded in 1469) had so increased by the end of the sixteenth century that its status had sunk considerably. As a result, King Henry III founded in 1578 a second, higher order whose membership was to be restricted to a hundred knights; this was the Order of the Holy Ghost. It was the first politically planned order which had a cross as its badge and not just the emblematic figure chosen in previous cases.

The number of orders having a more or less ornamented cross for their badge grew constantly, until finally the word "order" came to be generally applied to all cross-shaped badges.

The possibility of a sovereign's maintaining several different orders for different purposes was thoroughly exploited in France. In 1693 Louis XIV founded a military order of merit which was named after the French king St. Louis (reigned 1226–1270). It comprised the three grades which had also been maintained by the religious orders of knights: grand cross, commander, and knight. In 1759 it was complemented by a neutral order known simply as the Military

Order of Merit, since the Protestant officers—who included many Swiss—would not pay homage to St. Louis.

The concept of chivalrous organizations was not entirely extinguished, but it was hardly effective any longer. Plans

James of Savoy, Count of Romont, was lord of the Vaud from 1460 to 1486, and his arms are framed not by the Savoyard Order of the Annunciata, but by the French Order of the Camail, which had existed from 1394 to 1498 and is also called "The Porcupine." The letters *c* and *e* stand for *cominus* and *eminus* ("close to" and "at a distance").

to perpetuate the bodyguard of Emperor Constantine the Great (d. A.D. 337) in an Order of St. George under the grand mastership of a Byzantine prince in exile, and even to set up a company of soldiers to fight the Turks in Dalmatia, were never brought to fruition. Rather more successful was the founding of the Tuscan Order of St. Stephen in 1562, charged with the protection of Tuscan merchant shipping, as a result of which the battle flag of Tuscany showed a red cross on a white ground. The extensive collection of flags taken by the order from enemy ships hangs in the church of St. Stephen in Pisa.

The absolutist concept of the state produced some curious consequences. The foundation of new orders was painstakingly explained as a renewal of the ancient communities of knights, in order to give them a higher status. This was true especially of the Danish Danebrog Order, which in 1671 shifted its year of foundation back to 1219. Similarly the English Order of the Bath in 1725 traced its origin back to a supposed foundation of 1399.

To distinguish them from the

military orders, whose badge was and in some cases still is a large fabric cross borne on a cloak, the insignia of the courtly orders consisted of a symbolic figure which hung on a chain composed of several symbolically significant links. These orders on chains, some of which still exist, such as the Garter and the Golden Fleece, are the prototype of the numerous "chain" orders which are customarily used for the highest ranks of orders con-

taining several grades. The division of an order into several classes is the result of the abolition of the French military orders of merit with their maximum of three classes and their replacement by the *Légion d'honneur* in 1802. Its division into five classes became a model for most of the orders of merit awarded today.

The reaction against this, which is to divide an order into classes as little as possible or not at all, can be seen most clearly in the orders of the Soviet Union. There were no classes there until the Second World War, but the repeated award of the same decoration is permissible and has become constant practice.

A custom no longer adhered to but widely established during the last century was the inclusion in one's arms of decorations personally received. This

The knight Florian Waldauf of Waldenstein hangs the chain of his order on a ledge next to his armorial shield.

can be a valuable aid in dating works of art. The complete achievements of most European monarchies incorporate the higher classes of the orders of the country, as chain orders lend themselves particularly well to this purpose (see pages 38–39). Considerable historical interest attaches to the chapels of knightly orders, as in many countries their walls bear the arms of the members of the order, either during their lifetime or after their demise. In Great Britain the Orders of the Garter, the Bath, and St. Michael and St. George, the Order of the British Empire and of the Victoria Cross have their own churches with a display of armorial bearings, the last four of these in London, the Garter at Windsor, and the Scottish Order of the Thistle at Edinburgh.

Opposite top: Portrait of Heinrich Blarer from St. Gallen in 1460 wearing the sash of the Tankard Order of Aragon. The ornamental emblem with a griffin hanging on the wall also belongs to this order.

Center: In this portrait of the widely traveled Tirolean minnesinger Oswald von Wolkenstein (1377?– 1445), he wears the chain of the Tankard Order of Aragon and also its sash, to which he has added the Hungarian Order of the Dragon.

Above right: The portrait bust of Louis XIII of France solved the problem of how to wear the chains of two orders simultaneously. Here they are arranged concentrically. The superior order, that of the Holy Ghost, hangs deeper, while the other, that of St. Michael, has the shorter chain.

Right: St. Ambrose was venerated as the patron saint of Milan, which during a temporary period of independence from princely rule received the name "Ambrosian Republic" (1407 and 1447—1450).

Classical representation of the Holy Trinity as the symbolic arms of God himself.

During the classical period of heraldry, arms were even attributed to the unseen forces of the spirit. The Biblical prohibition against making images of God could easily be circumvented by representing the elusive concept of the Holy Trinity symbolically.

More frequently the instruments of the passion of Christ are represented on the escutcheon, or even distributed between the shield and crest in the form of an achievement of arms. A similar role might fall to saints, most notably in times when a throne had become vacant. The saints were then treated as the actual lords of the land, from whom the human sovereign had to hold his estates as it were in feudal tenure.

Apart from the cross of St. Andrew in Scotland, St. George in England, the three crowns of St. Eric in Sweden, and the apostolic cross of St. Stephen in Hungary, mention may be made of the arms assigned to saints from time to time, such as the birds gathered around the cross for Edward the Confessor, or the winged lion for St. Mark.

The arms of exotic king-doms as represented by central European compilers of arms collections in the fifteenth century; illustration from the *Chronicle of the Council of Constance*, 1483.

In the fourteenth and fifteenth centuries, people ascribed arms to every ancient prince or exotic kingdom which had been heard of. The arms of the king of Morocco consist of three chess pieces—they are rooks, which makes them canting in German (Moroc-co—*Maroch*; rook—*Roche*)—though Spanish sources show the whole chessboard instead of the single figures. The lions of Armenia with their small cross are based on genuine images on coins, and may have

become the arms of the Ethiopian empire as the symbol of the legendary Prester John. Philological interpretations of the constructions given by amateur blazons can often provide the solution for particular arms. This is true not only for armorials but also for ancestral arms on tombs which refer to generations far in the past. Much material on this subject is provided by Konrad Grünenberg, who had himself been to the Holy Land. From there he brought all kinds of fairy tales, including the belief that the great khan of the Tatars had a dog's head, since the name for dog is *canis*—unfortunately a Latin and not a Tatar word. Anyone who had been somewhere near Egypt and had heard talk of images of Anubis might well believe such erroneous tales. Discoveries related to whole kingdoms can of course be matched by discoveries relating to single prominent historical figures. This applies not only to such venerated figures as Charlemagne and others of the Nine Worthies, but also to the twins Romulus and Remus.

Far left: Symbolic arms of Death, an etching by Albrecht Dürer.

Implements of the passion of Christ as a papal sign of favor in a quarter of the banner of Schwyz, Switzerland, 1512.

The seals of the landgrave Conrad II of Thuringia around 1234; on the left-hand seal enthroned as ruler of his lands, on the other on horseback as leader of his army, in both cases bearing his armorial shield. As ruler, he shows the banner bestowed on him as a feudal lord; as leader of his troops he only required at the time a flag without an image on it—a gonfanon.

The Latin word for feudal tenure is *feudum*, a Germanic word with a Latin ending. It is probably formed from a Frankish word combination, *fehu-* (livestock) and *od* (movable possessions, property). This expresses the basic concept of feudal life, that the fief holder serves his feudal lord by means of his husbandry.

Feudal life, from an economic point of view, was both primitive and exclusive in nature. The economic aspect emerges clearly in another Latin word for feudal tenure, namely *beneficium*. The loyalty inherent in feudal life was thus based on two elements, one personal and one derived from necessity.

In the light of these two components, the early forms of heraldry become understandable. The idea of the inheritability of arms was only practicable after the feudal tenant had succeeded by constant effort in making the possessions entrusted to him during his lifetime transferable to his descendants.

Feudalism provided the basis of political development in the succession states of the Carolingian empire, and was the source of the arguments with which the kings of France gradually gained the upper

Charlemagne installs Roland as his representative in Spain and presents him with a gonfanon as a sign of sovereignty. He then takes his leave with a wave of the hand while Roland vainly tries to ram the staff of the banner into the rocky ground.

hand over their vassals. But in Germany this development took place in exactly the opposite manner. In 1180 the arrogant Duke of Bavaria and Saxony, Henry the Lion, was dispossessed of his imperial fief because of an offense against the duties of a vassal, although he retained the Guelph family estates. The emperor Frederick II made efforts to reorganize the German state on a feudal basis, with a whole hierarchy of loyalties. These efforts culminated in 1231 in the Statute of Favor of the Princes *(statutum in favorem principum)*. Its result was the division of Germany into innumerable territories.

A comparison can be made with the acquisition of lands

Das Reich Sicilia

Vernhart, Conig in Sicilia, Herzog zu Lotteringen und Baire, Marggraff Pomarancifel, zu Widelmoure Harrevery.

Das Reich Hungern

Das Reich ieronampso

Das Hertztom Lottring

Das marggrafftam pomarvanno

Die graffschafft Harabort

Die Vogallis

Die herschafft estletts

Two pages from the armorial of Jörg Rugenn (1495). In the middle of each is the achievement of arms of a sovereign (left, the king of Sicily and duke of Lorraine; right, the elector of Saxony). The subject lands and titles

by the conquering Normans in England in 1066. This was characterized by a total dispossession of the subjects and the transference of all land to the ownership of the new king, which with the help of feudalism led to the formation of a complete new upper stratum in society.

Arms were already customary in the time between the first and the second Crusades, and as the strict feudal conditions in the Crusader states demon-

possessed by these rulers are represented by the shields surrounding the central coat of arms. As yet there was some hesitation at dividing up the shield into a large number of quarters.

strate, as far as arms were concerned personal ties were decisive, and territorial ones only so when they were based on feudal law.

With the strengthening of sovereign power in the German empire, which was expressed also in the collection of several territories in one man's hands, the number of arms a single person was entitled to bear increased. This was the origin of the German princely arms with many quarterings.

The present-day arms of the cathedral city of Aix-la-Chapelle were thought to be those of Charlemagne throughout the Middle Ages. They consist of the arms of the Holy Roman Empire impaled with those of France.

Among the most interesting forms of heraldic research is that into the relationships which have produced an escutcheon of several different fields. In the beginning, that is to say from the first third of the twelfth century and for about a century afterward, the aim was to be as unequivocal as possible, so that there was no combining of several quarterings on one escutcheon. At the most, shields were halved or "impaled," giving rise to such curious figures as half eagles with lions butting onto them or bears with lions, back to back. Many examples of this are to be found in western Poland and also in Switzerland. The arms ascribed to Charlemagne are also formed in this way, though occasionally they show a whole or a double-headed eagle in the first quartering instead of a half eagle.

A significant event in the development of heraldry occurred in Spain. The heartland of Castile, together with the kingdom of León to the northwest, had not only carried the main burden of the *Reconquista*. Around 1230, the idea had arisen there of showing each coat of arms twice on a quartered shield. In this way the graphic presentation of the castle and the lion was hardly affected, and that only in the two lower quarterings. The example set a precedent and was probably taken up for the first time a century later in England. In 1337 King Edward III unleashed the so-called Hundred Years' War and adopted the title of "king of France," giving it precedence over his own title as the king of England. On his arms he imitated the Spanish method of combining the arms of two states on a quartered shield, with France taking

The oldest arms of the Swedish state are simultaneously those of the Folkunger dynasty (the

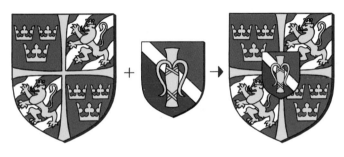

lion on a wavy field). The three crowns have been accepted as the actual arms of the country since the fourteenth century. From the fifteenth century it was the custom to bear the arms of the ruling dynasty inescutcheon. After Gustavus Wasa, the leader of a national uprising, was chosen as Gustavus I, King of Sweden, in 1523, this system was continued.

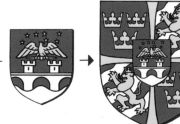

precedence over England. From then on quartered arms grew increasingly in popularity. In the *Armorial de Gelre* there are almost exactly a hundred, among 1707 entries. Up to the fifteenth century arms with more than four quarterings were avoided; people preferred to quarter one of the fields again. The decisive steps away from quartering in the arrangement of fields seem to have been taken in the fifteenth century by King René le Bon and by the archdukes of Austria.

The technically possible combinations of arms are, then, as follows:

1. The two shields of a married couple, on which an inheritance is based, are placed side by side, particularly during their lifetime.

2. The two armorial bearings are placed side by side on a divided shield without alteration of their contents, but in such a way as to fit the altered shape of the background.

3. Half of each of the two armorial bearings is combined on a divided shield (impalement).

4. One of the two armorial bearings suited to it is halved, while the other remains unchanged.

5. The two armorial bearings are combined on a quartered shield so that the senior coat appears in the first and fourth quarters, and the less important in the second and third quarters.

6. If further armorial bearings are to be introduced, they can be given a place in an inescutcheon shield which may be regarded as the best or the least significant position according to circumstances.

The arms of the kingdom of the Two Sicilies are the most complicated of the Capetian arms ever devised. The basis is provided by the combination of the arms of Spain (quarters 1–5 in the diagram below) and Austria-Burgundy (6–11), to which the arms of the house of Bourbon-Anjou (14) were added in 1701.

After the Spanish *Infante* Charles (b. 1716) had succeeded his great-uncle Anthony as duke of Parma and Piacenza in 1731, he conquered Naples in 1734 and was recognized there as King Charles VII. Having renounced the dukedom of Parma, he was then invested by the pope with Sicily and the kingdom of Jerusalem in 1738.

He retained all the quarters inherited from his father (1–11

One of the most significant marriages in world history was that in 1477 between Archduke Maximilian of Austria and Marie, the heiress of the dukedom of Burgundy. In the new seal of the ruling couple most of their arms are combined in a compatible way; however, in the arms of Maximilian the central shields are brought together and their order changed, so that the

Tyrol appears in the Burgundian quarter and Flanders in the Austrian quarter.

Demolished in 1766, the armorial tower in Innsbruck *(left)* was painted in 1497 with the arms of all the Hapsburg subject territories, right down to the very smallest in Flanders (e.g., Aalst) and the Grisons (e.g., Rhäzüns).

227

Simplified form of the arms of the Two Sicilies.

Right: Arms of the Kingdom of the Two Sicilies.

In the diagram shown here, the different quarters are numbered in accordance with the nineteen shields on pages 230–231, to facilitate reference. Quarters 1 to 11 had already

and 14) and added beneath them quarters 12 and 13 for the kingdom won in 1735. At the sides were added the arms of Parma (15–18) and Medici (19) derived from his mother Elizabeth (Isabel Farnese).

When he unexpectedly inherited the throne of Spain form his half-brother Ferdinand VI in 1759, quarters 12 and 13 were removed, but 15 and 19 were included in the arms of succession.

As second wife of Philip V, the first Bourbon king of Spain, Queen Elizabeth (Isabel) had no hope of her children succeeding to the throne of Spain, but had successfully managed to provide them with other states. She brought with her the claim not only to Parma but also to Tuscany.

As a result of the marriage of Duke Octavio with a daughter of Emperor Charles V, the arms of the dukedom of Parma had consisted since 1556 of a combination of the arms of the house of Farnese with the Austrian-Burgundian arms and the attribute of the papal standard-bearer. The son of this marriage, Alexander (d. 1592) had married Maria, a daughter of the pretender to the vacant throne of Portugal, and could therefore hold out

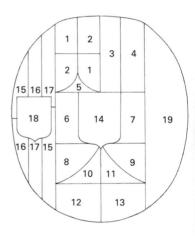

been borne by the emperor Charles V (King Charles I of Spain). The inescutcheon was added when a grandson of the French king Louis XIV became king of Spain. The addition of all the remaining quarters created the arms of a kingdom which existed until 1867. Quarters 15 to 19 persisted until 1931 in the arms of the Spanish state.

229

1 CASTILE

Gules, a castle or with gate and windows azure (canting arms).

2 LEÓN

Argent, a lion gules (originally purpure) crowned or (also canting arms).

3 ARAGON

Paly of nine or and gules, really the arms of the county of Barcelona (= Catalonia).

4 SICILY

Quartered per saltire of Aragon and Hohenstaufen (argent, an eagle sable).

5 GRANADA

Argent, a pomegranate with leaves, proper (canting arms).

6 AUSTRIA

Gules, a fess argent (see number 16).

7 NEW BURGUNDY

Within a bordure compony gules and argent, azure, semy-de-lis or.

8 OLD BURGUNDY

Within a bordure gules, bendy of six or and azure.

9 BRABANT

Sable, a lion or; the present-day arms of Belgium.

10 FLANDERS

Or, a lion sable; today the arms of the Belgian province of Eastern Flanders.

11 TYROL

Argent, an eagle gules crowned or, wings surmounted with trefoils on stems or.

12 OLD ANJOU (the kingdom of Naples)

Azure, semy-de-lis or, with a label of five points gules.

In 1545 Pope Paul III (d. 1549) of the house of Farnese appointed his illegitimate son Peter Louis duke of Parma and "Standard bearer of the Church" *(Gonfaloniere della*

Chiesa). In his coat of arms the badge of the Gonfaloniere, the papal umbrella (far right), appeared between the six fleurs-de-lis of Parma. In 1538 Peter Louis's son married an illegitimate daughter of the emperor Charles V, Margaret (1522—1586), who like the other imperial children bore a simple coat of arms consisting of the shield of Austria (16) impaled with that of Old Burgundy (17). She became known historically as the unfortunate governor general of the Spanish Netherlands, installed in 1559.

13 KINGDOM OF JERUSALEM

Argent, a cross potent or, cantoned of four crosses or.

14 NEW ANJOU

Azure, within a bordure gules, three fleurs-de-lis or.

15 PARMA (FARNESE)

Or, six fleurs-de-lis azure (3, 2, 1); really the family arms of the house of Farnese.

16 AUSTRIA

See number 6. Often the coat of arms for all Hapsburg territories before 1477.

17 OLD BURGUNDY

Bendy of six or and azure (see number 8); bordure often omitted in Austria.

18 PORTUGAL

Within a bordure gules surmounted by seven castles or, the so-called quinas.

19 TUSCANY (MEDICI)

Or, six balls (1, 2, 2, 1), the five lower ones gules, the uppermost azure surmounted with three fleurs-de-lis or.

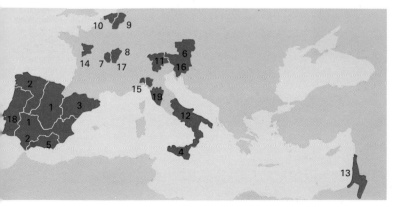

The map indicates the areas whose arms were incorporated in the arms of the kingdom of the Two Sicilies.

The numbers relate to the diagram on page 228.

231

some hope of his son Ranuncio I becoming king of Portugal. For this reason the latter incorporated the Portuguese shield as inescutcheon in the arms of Parma. The office of papal standard-bearer lapsed with the excommunication of Odoardo in 1641 and the corresponding badge of office had to be removed. The quarters of Farnese and Austria-Burgundy, previously kept apart in the quartering, were now rearranged into six quarters of the same size.

In countries where the French Salic law restricting the succession to the male line did not apply and women were allowed to succeed to the throne, as in England and Castile, the bearing of arms by women was naturally more frequent than elsewhere. Thus in England complicated rules were developed for the combination of marriage arms and arms of widowhood, from which the status of widowers also can be established. According to these rules, a woman's arms are borne not on a shield but on a lozenge, a convention which did not establish itself in central Europe and which makes the rendering of somewhat complicated armorial bearings very difficult.

The heraldically expressed alliance need not necessarily be a marriage. A business partnership, such as that of the incunabula printers Fust and Schöffer, can equally well be expressed by shields turned toward one another, as can a combination of several territorial or official arms.

Basically, the arms to dexter, which are normally those of the higher ranking partner—in marriages, therefore, those of the man—should be inclined toward the arms of the other partner out of courtesy, though this is often not the case for a variety of reasons.

Two armorial shields may also be placed side by side in the case of city-states such as Nuremberg, especially those which for some reason have two different sets of arms.

This figure is on the side panel of a triptych by Lucas van Leyden, the center of which represents *The Healing of the Blind Man*. The young woman carries the lozenge shield customary for her sex in the Netherlands.

ECCLESIASTICAL HERALDRY

Church heraldry has two individual characteristics. Most notable is the omission of the helmet, with its military associations. On the other hand, the shield, also derived from military equipment, remains uncontested as the basis of the arms of ecclesiastical dignitaries. Instead of the helmet and crest, ecclesiastical insignia are used. These include the broad-brimmed pilgrim's hat, with different colors and arrangements of tasseled cords to denote rank, also the shepherd's crook, with or without a sudarium, and the processional cross, sometimes with two or even three crosspieces. A striving for greater simplicity in the last few decades has led to the less frequent use of insignia, especially the miter, by some prelates of the Roman Catholic faith. The miter was once much used by archbishops, bishops, and abbots to ensign their arms.

The pope is the only church dignitary who bears a crown, the so-called papal tiara—also known as the *triregnum;* he places it on or above his armorial shield.

Arms of Pope John Paul II
(1978–   ).

The hierarchy of the Church is expressed heraldically in the gradations of head coverings in ecclesiatical arms. Recently an effort has been made to show only one type of headgear, preferably the broadbrimmed hat with tassels *(fiocchi)* denoting rank by their number and color.

Left, top to bottom:

CARDINAL (30 red tassels).

PATRIARCH (30 green tassels), also bailiff of the Maltese Order of the Knights of St. John.

ARCHBISHOP (20 green tassels), also knight grand cross of the Order of the Holy Sepulcher.

Right, top to bottom:

BISHOP (12 green tassels).

EXEMPT ABBEY. The bishop's insignia are accompanied by the crozier with sudarium and the sword.

ABBESS. Family arms in the German style surmounting the arms of the convent (a Cistercian one), with a crozier behind the shield.

235

ARMORIAL BEARINGS
OF UNIVERSITIES

Many universities have only
the seal essential for the
ratification of documents,
usually with some kind of
symbolic image.

UNIVERSITY
OF MARBURG

UNIVERSITY
OF SALZBURG
UNTIL 1962

UNIVERSITY
OF OXFORD

UNIVERSITY
OF CAMBRIDGE

EDINBURGH
UNIVERSITY

The word university is derived from *Universitas litterarum,* which means generality of knowledge. Obviously, in order to be able to organize this generality, a university must be institutionalized, and as such it will need to bear a genuine seal.

Since there is nowhere in the world where universities serve directly military ends, their relationship with heraldry depends on external, intellectual considerations. The picture on the seal can be a heraldic or a non-heraldic motif, or both together.

The armorials of the Middle Ages and from the beginning of modern times contain many university arms which are based on a combination of the regional arms with the symbol of learning, a book. The extent to which these were transferred to seals depended on individual circumstances. As was the case with many towns, the seals developed independently of the arms. Combinations such as that of Salzburg are very frequent, and in English-speaking countries genuine arms are commonly used.

UNIVERSITY
OF SALZBURG
SINCE 1972

FREE UNIVERSITY
OF BERLIN

British culture created academic institutions in all areas of British influence, as for example in Grahamstown, Natal, South Africa *(bottom left)*.

A tendency to express modern scientific discoveries in heraldic terms can be found among the

TRINITY
COLLEGE (IRELAND)

HARVARD
UNIVERSITY

YALE
UNIVERSITY

younger universities. An example is offered by the wave forms and the symbol of an atomic nucleus in the arms of the University of Warwick *(below)*.

PATRICIAN REPUBLICS

The use of the distinction between a monarchy and a republic to describe the constitution of a state has largely been replaced in the present day by the distinction between democracy and dictatorship. But until the end of the eighteenth century it remained fully valid. As a result of the ruling" which in many places had to defend themselves against the up-and-coming tradesmen's guilds. The city-states in Italy, Switzerland,

feudally-based policies of the Hohenstaufen emperors, the towns known as republics up to that time had acquired an autonomy unimaginable to communities lying outside the German Roman empire. This autonomy had little to do with democracy, since it was exercised by "families capable of and to a certain extent Germany, created subject territories for themselves and justified their status by reference to feudal lords whose titles had ceased to have any significance. Their arms seldom go back to the images on seals, being more often derived from military banners. This is the

The arms of the powerful republic of Venice *(below)* include the emblems of the territories it ruled as far as Cyprus. On top of the armorial tent is the fisherman's cap, the badge of ducal rank of the doge (i.e., duke).

The magic word *Libertas* ("freedom") accompanied the Italian city-states through the centuries, and in the case of San Marino has even maintained its value to the present day. Both the arms of Ragusa (Dubrovnik) and of Bologna express the old will to independence.

Above: Arms of Genoa, with a king's crown which was added above the shield, with the red cross of its patron St. George, after the acquisition of the kingdom of Corsica.

Far left: Arms of the city of Lucca, 1835. The form is that in which they were borne by the town during the time of its independence, with the addition of the ducal medal of merit.

Left: The independent status of the Swiss cantons was expressed by a crown of sovereignty on their coats of arms. An example is Bern, whose state seal, engraved in 1768, is shown here.

case with the Swiss cantons of Zurich, Lucerne, Fribourg, and Solothurn, whose arms consist of simple ordinaries, and Lucca and Siena in Italy. The cross of Genoa and the figure of St. Blaise of Ragusa (Dubrovnik) demonstrate the subjection of these places to a local spiritual figure.

The arms of the former sovereigns are recalled by the pales of Foix and Catalonia and the cows of Béarn, as well as the

239

The desire for independence from the power of the local sovereign was accompanied by the belief in the protective power of a patron saint. In Ragusa (Dubrovnik), St. Blaise was venerated for this reason. A flag bearing his image flew from a high mast in the market square. The unusually large merchant fleet of Ragusa bore his picture or initials or the word *Libertas* on their white flags.

bend in the canting arms of Bern, since the founder of the latter city was an ancestor of the margraves of Baden (whose arms were: or, a bend gules).

An example of genuine arms of sovereignty is offered by those of the Republic of Venice, which are formed from quarters of Venetia and the Adriatic coastal territories of Istria and Croatia, with Dalmatia and Rascia and the islands of Zante and Cyprus.

EGALITARIAN REPUBLICS

New England revolutionary flag, 1775.

To the innovator the rules of heraldry are irrelevant, even if he cannot do without the symbolism. The separation of the American colonies from Great Britain was symbolized by the tree which free peoples used as a place of assembly and judgment even in ancient times. The spruce appeared on the flag of New England as early as 1686.

The tree was also the symbol of the French Revolution, and men who had "freed" themselves from the aristocratic oppressors danced round trees of liberty decorated with the colors of France and with the cap of liberty placed on top. A general enthusiasm for the model of the republic of ancient Rome led to the adoption of its symbolism as well—women in flowing garments with the fasces of the lictors, bound sheaves of arrows, cornucopias, and Phrygian caps. Switzerland, which was then called the Helvetian Republic following the French model, reached rather less far back into its own store of traditions. In William Tell the Swiss found their own indigenous symbol of defiance.

With this anti-heraldic style of emblem, tricolor flags and banderoles came to be almost synonymous with republicanism, and legitimists therefore adopted two-color combinations. The Commonwealth of the Lord Protector Oliver Cromwell from 1649 to 1658 and of his son Richard, bearing the same title from 1658 to 1660, is the prototype of those non-monarchic states which in their choice of symbols cling

When in 1918 the crown was removed from German coats of arms, the arms themselves were spared where possible (*left,* Oldenburg; *right,* Württemberg).

241

In the last decades of the eighteenth century the tree, a symbol of self-government, became the emblem of republican freedom in Europe and of the rejection of English tutelage in America.

closely to history. Only openly monarchic emblems are brought into question. If these are unmistakable emblems of rank, such as imperial crowns, then their days are clearly numbered. But ornamental crowns, declared to be "people's crowns" and a sign of the sovereignty of component states, have often overcome understandable prejudices against them, as in the case of Bavaria, Hessen, Baden-Württemberg, the Rhineland Palatinate, and with modifications, West Berlin. One of the oldest republics of the nineteenth century, the Spanish republic of 1868, adopted the mural crown in its meaning as a citizens' crown, an example followed by the republic of Austria.

The republican form of state, which in nineteenth-century Europe was as yet an exception, became widely established after the end of the First World War. The downfall of small and large monarchies in Germany everywhere created the problem of how the insignia of the new states were to be

LOI
du 26 Juillet
1798.

RÉPUBLIQUE HELVÉTIQUE
UNE ET INDIVISIBLE
CANTON DE BÂLE

constituted. In general, the coats of arms borne by the local rulers were retained, even though these were almost always their family arms.

The people's or socialist republics, with their more all-embracing republican attitude, have rather more difficulty in maintaining tradi-

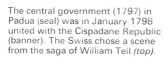

The central government (1797) in Padua (seal) was in January 1798 united with the Cispadane Republic (banner). The Swiss chose a scene from the saga of William Tell *(top)*.

tions. Some of them have been able to retain a link with the past; the socialist republic of Czechoslovakia has even done so by using a form of shield that is considered typical.

243

Town air makes free, says an old German proverb. But for this to be possible the town itself must be free, and free from royal sovereignty. The connection appears clearly in the community seals of the large medieval towns on which the patron saints are represented, sometimes in scenes of martyrdom, and sometimes characterized by their attributes and framed by buildings which form a portrait of the town.

Development of the municipal arms of Mainz *(upper row):* Seal of 1392. Initial from around 1440. Napoleonic armorial letter, 1811.

Arms after the fall of Napoleon Arms granted in 1915. Medal of the "good cities," commemorating the birth of the king of Rome, 1811 *(far right).*

These seals are not, however, the forerunners of the municipal arms, although there are many such arms which can be traced back to images of

saints. There is no truly unanimous view as to whether a municipal coat of arms should consist of ornamental emblems in addition to the shield. Many old and important towns complete the arms with a helmet and crest. Others add crowns of one kind or another. By far the most common are mural crowns going back to antiquity which the three most important German imperial towns, Nuremberg, Augsburg, and Frankfurt, placed on their shield at the

The seals above show a selection of municipal motifs.

Reverse of a gold seal of the emperor Ludwig of Bavaria with a bird's eye view of Rome, 1328.

Back of a seal of King Baldwin I of Jerusalem (1118–1131) with the representation of the three most important buildings in this "city of the king of kings."

Great seal of Hamburg, 1254, model for the official seal of 1864.

Municipal seal of Emmerich (Lower Rhine) with the stylized representation of a town and above it shields with the canting arms of the town (pails = *Eimer*), 1237.

Back of the seal of the town of Arles (southern France) with the image of the town's patron saint and representatives of the guilds forming the municipal government.

beginning of the eighteenth century. These crowns have become widespread since the nineteenth century, although in Germany they have been

falsely suspected of being an inheritance of the despised Napoleonic heraldry.

There has been a widespread tendency in Europe over the last few decades to create arms for every community and not only for those which carry the title of a town. Thus even in democratically governed countries, there is scarcely a community which does not have its own arms.

This gallery of the arms of such capitals as have them, supplemented by a few further major towns, will give us a rapid survey of the kind of elements used to make up municipal arms.

Since Reykjavik created a coat of arms for itself in 1957, Athens is the sole European capital which has only a seal, showing the goddess Athene. Moscow is left out of consideration because its historical arms go against the current political attitude, and a provisional coat of arms dating from 1925 has fallen out of use. Moreover, the current movement in the Soviet Union to provide new arms which conform with the system has achieved results in towns such as Kiev, Odessa, Sochi, Saporoshje, Riga, Stalingrad, and others, but has not yet affected Moscow. Historic arms such as those of Novgorod are still occasionally to be found.

Ancient tradition lives on in the letters SPQR *(Senatus Populus Que Romanus*—the Roman senate and people), which are found on arms dating back to the Middle Ages. Also of medieval origin are the armorial cross of the Crusader port of Marseilles, the Guel-phic cross of Milan, and the German cross of Vienna.

The canting arms with bears of Berlin and Bern are very old, as is the city of London's cross of St. George with the sword of St. Paul. The castles in the arms of Bratislava (Pressburg) and Hamburg can be traced back to old municipal seals; today they are drawn in a more modern fashion, whereas the castle of Prague sticks closely to Hussite prototypes.

The arms of Naples are probably based on figures from medieval banners, those of Zurich definitely so. Examples of coats of arms based on local mythology are the very old arms of Warsaw showing a mermaid, and the newly constituted arms of Reykjavik showing the traditional throne supports of the Vikings immersed in water.

Almost all the arms of capitals of former colonies are newly created, and in the English-speaking area most have been granted by the English kings of arms. This is a continuation of an old Spanish tradition, for in the sixteenth century Spain bestowed a coat of arms on many of her former colonies.

ABIDJAN

ALGIERS

AMSTERDAM

ASUNCIÓN

ATHENS

BAMAKO

BANJUL

BELFAST

BELGRADE

BERLIN

BERN

BOGOTÁ

BONN

BRATISLAVA

BRAZZAVILLE

BRUSSELS

BUCHAREST

BUDAPEST

BUENOS AIRES

CANBERRA

CARACAS

CASABLANCA

CHICAGO

DAKAR

DELHI

DEN HAAG

DUBLIN

EDINGBURGH

FRANKFURT-
AM-MAIN

GENEVA

GUANABARA

GUATEMALA

HAMBURG

HELSINKI

JERUSALEM

KAMPALA

KINGSTON

KINSHASA

COPENHAGEN

KYOTO

248

LAGOS

LA HABANA
(HAVANA)

LA PAZ

LIBREVILLE

LIMA

LISBON

LONDON

LOS ANGELES

LUANDA

LUXEMBOURG

LYON

MADRID

MANILA

MARSEILLES

MEXICO
CITY

MILAN

MONACO

MONTEVIDEO

MONTREAL

MOSCOW

NAIROBI

NAPLES

N'DJAMENA

NEW YORK

OSAKA

OSLO

OTTAWA

PANAMA

PARIS

PORT-AU-PRINCE

PRAGUE

PRETORIA

QUEBEC

QUITO

RANGOON

REIMS

REYKJAVIK

ROME

SALISBURY

SAN FRANCISCO

SAN JOSÉ DE COSTA RICA

SAN MARINO

SANTA ISABEL

SANTIAGO DE CHILE

SANTO DOMINGO

SEOUL

SINGAPORE

SOFIA

STOCKHOLM

TANANARIVE

TOKYO

TORONTO

VADUZ

WARSAW

WASHINGTON

WELLINGTON

WIEN (VIENNA)

WINDHOEK

WINNIPEG

ZURICH

Death and burial have been the occasion for solemn ceremonies and have been recorded in pictorial form since time immemorial. The higher a man's rank in the world, the greater his need to leave evidence of his importance for posterity. Powerful men order their tombs far in advance of their death. As a result their heirs then frequently forget to add the date of death when the time comes.

Many have confined the decoration of their tombs to a portrayal of themselves in full figure, dressed in clothing or in armor. Where possible they had this figure accompanied by the arms of their parents and grandparents and even other more distant generations. It was fairly unusual, however, to show the mourners on one's tomb, even as supporters for the ancestral arms. Among the higher nobility, those in the funeral procession often acted as bearers of the ancestral or other arms. The funeral banners, usually black and painted with the ancestral arms, were then hung up in the church where the corpse was buried, and here, eaten away by the black coloring, they slowly disintegrated. This could be avoided by the use of more durable material such as

The knight Hans von Bischofswerder appears on his fifteenth-century gravestone, in the church at Ebersbach near Görlitz, framed by the eight coats of arms of his ancestors.

Philippe Pot, Grand Seneschal of Burgundy, chamberlain to King Louis XI of France and governor of Burgundy, commissioned his own tomb in 1493, shortly before his death. The mourners carry the escutcheons of seven of his great-grandparents; the mother of the mother of his father being unknown, he placed his family arms (or, a fess azure) in the eighth position to fill the gap. The mourner at the head end (on the right) bears the augmentation in a canton added by Philippe's grandfather Regnier, in memory of the fact that during a campaign against the heathenish Prussians in 1389 he was awarded the heroic name of Palamades. Paris, Musée du Louvre.

wooden boards, which in Sweden are still known as funeral banners in memory of the material they replaced.

Funeral procession of Queen Elizabeth I of England, 1603. The dead queen or her likeness lies in state on the sarcophagus, surrounded by the twelve banners of her forebears. The first is that of Henry II, married in 1152 to Eleanor of Aquitaine; beneath it John (of no estates), married in 1200 to Isabel of Angoulême. The next pair, Henry III, 1236 married to Eleanor of Provence; Edward I, 1254 to Eleanor of Castile. Edward II, 1308 to Isabel of France; Edward III, 1328 to Philippa of Hainault. Edmund Langley, Duke of York, 1372 to Isabel of Castile; Richard, Earl of Cambridge, to Anne Mortimer from the house of the earls of March.
The four banners not shown:
Richard, Duke of York, 1438 to Cecily Neville; Edward IV, 1464 to Elizabeth Woodville. Elizabeth, a daughter of this royal marriage, 1468 to Henry VII; and finally Henry VIII to Anne Boleyn, the marriage which produced Queen Elizabeth I.

iott drawne by foure Horses vpon whic
Coffin couered w'th purple Veluett and
representation, The Canapy borne by six

Contemporary artists have often left very exact illustrated records of the solemn processions. They provide valuable historical documentation both of the costumes worn and of the arms and banners used at the time. The banners which accompanied Queen Elizabeth I of England to the grave bore the arms of her forefathers over twelve gener-

ations. (See the illustration above.)

Elizabeth's funeral procession was further decorated with the dead queen's arms on the horse trappers, surrounded by the emblem of the Order of the Garter. On their heads and cruppers the horses also carried pennants with the initials and the badges of Elizabeth I.

PICTURE CREDITS

Page

es, Paris. Sun emblem.
– Spain. Drawings by Coray.
200a Italy, from *Freiburg Book of Colors,*
Freiburg State Archives. Photo:
Benedikt Rast, Freiburg.
200r Milan, Biblioteca Trivulziana,
Cod. 1390.
201 Milan, Biblioteca Trivulziana,
Cod. 2168.
202 B.N.; ms. français 2313, fol. 394.
203l B.N.; ms. français 854, fol. 113v.
203r Oe, N.; Cod. 2606, fol. 70v.
204 Stockholm, Kungl. Livrustkam-
maren.
205 Frederiksborg Castle. Photo: Poul
Ainow, Copenhagen.
206 Marburg, Church of St. Elisabeth,
west portal.
206r Heraldry of Nicholas von Diesbach. B.H.M.
207 From *Geschichte des ritterlichen Johan-
niter Ordens,* Justus Christoph Dith-
mar. Frankfurt a. Oder, 1728.
208–209 l to r:
– *Geschichte der Preussischen Münzen
und Siegel,* F.A. Vossberg, Berlin,
1842, pl. 1 no. 6.
– Foto Picture Library, Marburg.
– Author's tracing from Gelre.
– From Vossberg cf. above, pl. XI.
208c/l Author's tracing from Gelre.
208c/r Publisher.
208b No. 9863, photographic service of
the Archives Nationales, Paris.
209c/l Ex Libris designed by B.B.
Heim. © B.B. Heim and Van
Duren Publishers, reproduced from
Archbishop Heim's definitive work
Heraldry in the Catholic Church
(Van Duren Publishers), Gerrards
(cross) by kind permission of the
publisher.
209c/r Publisher.
209b From *Österreichisch-ungarisch Wap-
penrolle,* H.G. Ströhl, Vienna, 1894.
210 From *Abbildungen und Beschreibung
aller hohen Ritter-Orden in Europa,* G.
Lichter, Augsburg, 1759.
212 Nuremberg, G.N.M.; Gm 581.
213 Basel Art Museum.
214r Constance, Rosgarten Museum.
214b Municipal Museum of Solbad
Hall; now stored in Innsbruck, Ty-
rolian Regional Museum.
215l Innsbruck University Library.
215r Paris, Louvre.
216l Otto Hupp, from the copy in Maria Hupp collection, Oberschleiss-
heim.
217 *Freiburg Book of Colors,* Freiburg
State Archives.

218–219 From C.C.C.
218b/l Schweinfurt, Otto Schäfer collection, D-98.
218b/r Schwyz Federal Document Archives. Photo: James Perret.
220a Wolfenbüttel, State Archives.
221 St. Gallen, Municipal Library.
222–223 Innsbruck, University Library.
223, 224 Drawings: Franz Coray.
227l Printed sheet, 19th century.
227r From *Sigilla comitus Flandriae Oli-
varius Vradius,* Brussels, 1639.
228, 229 Drawings: Franz Coray.
230l From D.W.W., pl. 15.
230r Drawings: Author F. Coray.
231a/l From D.W.W., pl. 15.
231a/r, 231b Author and F. Coray.
232 Leningrad, Hermitage. Photo:
Novosti Press Agency, Geneva.
234, 235 Seven illustrations © B.B.
Heim and Van Duren Publishers.
The coat of arms of Pope John
Paul II was designed by Archbishop Heim. These illustrations
are reproduced from his definitive
work *Heraldry in the Catholic Church*
(Van Duren Publishers), Gerrards
(cross) by kind permission of the
publisher.
236–237a Official designs, Publisher.
238 Drawing: Franz Coray, Lucerne.
238b/l Author. Photo: Cortopassi.
238b/r Bern, State Archives. Photo:
Hugo Frutig, Bern.
239 From *Illustrazione Storica dello stemma
di Genova,* A. Boscassi, Genua, 1919.
239b From D.W.W., pl. 21.
240 Dubrovnik, Dominican church.
Photo: André Held, Ecublens.
241a Publisher.
241b From *Die Wappen und Flaggen des
Deutschen Reichs und der Deutschen
Länder,* Berlin, 1928, pls. VII, IV.
242 Photo: Benziger Verlag, Zurich.
243a Bern, Swiss National Library.
243b/l Museo Bottacin.
243b/r Author.
244–245 Munich, State Coin Coll.
– Seal Jerusalem/Publisher.
– Hamburg, State Archives.
– Düsseldorf, Main State Archives
– Seal of Arles. Author.
244b Mainz, Municipal Archives
245 Photo: Musée Monétaire, Paris.
247–249 Publisher.
250–251 *Brockhaus Encyclopädie.*
252–253b Details in *Cahiers d'Héraldique*
II, Paris 1975, pp. 179–212. Photo:
M.N.P.
253 From *Der Deutsche Herold,* 1927.
254–255 B.L. ms. Add. 35 324, fol. 37v.

INDEX